*Manufacturing
in the Ottoman Empire and Turkey,
1500–1950*

SUNY Series in the Social and Economic History
of the Middle East
Donald Quataert, editor

Manufacturing
in the Ottoman Empire and Turkey,
1500–1950

Edited by
Donald Quataert

State University of New York Press

Published by
State University of New York Press, Albany

For information, address State University of New York Press,
State University Plaza, Albany, N.Y. 12246

Production by Cindy Tenace Lassonde
Marketing by Fran Keneston

Library of Congress Cataloging-in-Publication Data

Manufacturing in the Ottoman Empire and Turkey, 1500–1950 / edited by
Donald Quataert.
    p.   cm. — (SUNY series in the social and economic history of
the Middle East)
  Includes bibliographical references and index.
  ISBN 0-7914-2015-9 (alk. paper). — ISBN 0-7914-2016-7 (pbk. :
alk. paper)
   1. Turkey—Manufactures—History. 2. Turkey—Economic conditions.
  3. Turkey—History—Ottoman Empire, 1288–1918. I. Quataert, Donald, 1941–
II. Series.
HD9736.T92M36   1994
338.4'767'09561--dc20   93-36571
                                                                 CIP

10 9 8 7 6 5 4 3 2 1

To Laurie
D. Q.

Contents

Tables

Introduction

Donald Quataert

In many respects, the present volume marks the continuing maturation of Ottoman and Turkish studies. First of all, it is a departure from the stress that has been placed on the agrarian sector of the Ottoman economy. This emphasis, I hasten to add, certainly has been appropriate. After all, the Ottoman state was an agrarian empire in which most people lived in the countryside and gained at least part of their livelihoods from the soil. And, most state revenues were extracted from the agrarian sector. A volume devoted to manufacturing hardly indicates that research on Ottoman/Turkish agriculture has been exhausted; quite the opposite is the case. But it does suggest a certain broadening of the historical inquiry regarding the nature and evolution of the Ottoman economy and an emerging ability to move beyond the most basic issues. At a fundamental level, the present volume demonstrates that more than primary production was taking place within the frontiers of this agrarian state. That is, the actual complexity of the Ottoman economy is now just beginning to be reflected in the historical scholarship.

In yet a second manner, this volume underscores positive developments in Ottoman and Middle Eastern studies. Versions of the four contributions that follow originally were presented at a conference, sponsored by the Southwest Asian and North African program and the Fernand Braudel Center, held at the State University of New York-

Binghamton, in November 1990. The conference was an unusual, even extraordinary, experience for many of its participants. Untypically, the four Ottoman/Turkish experts presented their research findings not to colleagues in the same area of specialization, but to scholars whose expertise lay in other areas of the world.[1] At the conference, specialists in various other regions—i.e., the United States, Italy, China, India, and Latin America—read and commented, in extenso, on one of the Ottoman/Turkish manufacturing papers. The intermingling of scholars of the varying recondite fields, in this age of academic over-specialization, forced the participants—presenters and commentators alike—to abandon their code languages and signals. This was a heady, and mutually enriching, experience.

Aficionados of the Ottoman past certainly gained from the encounter. At a very basic level, the comparisons with other regions reminded us of important realities affecting the industrial sector in quite fundamental ways. Take, for example, the mere size of the domestic market. While India and China during the nineteenth century each held 300 to 400 million potential domestic consumers, the Ottoman lands contained but twenty to twenty-five million![2] Thus, the comparative approach takes the specificities of the Ottoman case, which often have obscured the outline and meaning of those historical experiences, and use them to offer us new questions to ask and new perspectives to employ. While comparative history certainly does not have all the answers, it seems especially useful for underdeveloped fields of inquiry such as Ottoman and Turkish and, more generally, Middle Eastern studies. For example, the Ottoman/Turkish specialists who had uncovered rural manufacturing in their own research took courage from the commentators' repeated observations that manufacturing in the countryside also was commonplace and important in areas as diverse as the nineteenth-century United States and eighteenth-century India. The comparative approach thus made abundantly clear that cultivators all over the world very often not only tilled fields but also manufactured goods for sale as well. Globally, manufacturing has not been and is not now simply an urban endeavor. And more, the commentators emphasized the close links between rural and urban production, as towns often finished country manufactures. Thus, they encouraged us to look more closely for such patterns in the Middle Eastern lands.

The conference reinforced my own belief that the field of Ottoman and Middle Eastern studies has made few, if any, methodological contributions to the major debates taking place in the fields of history and economic history. Why this is so is not clear.[3] Part of the answer certainly lies in the tendency of Ottoman historians to focus on one or another part of that once-vast empire. We too often do not treat the Ottoman economy in its entirety but rather study it in fragmentary form. Thus, we learn more about the subregions and less about the complex unity of the whole economy. Some of us have become specialists on the Turkish areas, others focus on the Arab or the Bulgarian regions. In our own defense, we specialists quickly point to the linguistic difficulties that indeed are real: Serbo-Croatian or Greek gives way to Bulgarian and to Turkish and to Arabic or Armenian, depending on the region. Many of these languages are difficult to acquire and there is some truth to this defense. But, the political division of the post-Ottoman Middle East into its southeast European, Turkish, and Arab nation-state components probably is a more important factor than mere linguistics. Although these regions have a shared economic history, their historiographies have remained nearly completely distinct because their historians, by and large, have adopted the agendas of the various states formed out of the debris of the Ottoman Empire. Thus, for example, historians in the various Balkan successor states too often battle their nationalist movements' Ottoman scourge. Those focusing on Turkey mirror the *étatist* biases and fears of the Turkish republican elites and worry overmuch about the state and its economic role. Surely a first step towards a methodological improvement of Ottoman studies is to reintegrate the regions of analysis into the single unit they once were.

Another source of methodological backwardness is our ignorance of the actual Ottoman historical experiences. Because the field of Ottoman studies is relatively new and very small, we often do not know what happened in the past. There are few researchers despite the centrality of Ottoman history for an understanding of Europe and the Middle East throughout the early modern and modern periods. The absence of even a basic framework of facts obviously impedes our understanding of their significance. While this excuse often is marshalled to avoid intellectual rigor, the absence of researchers remains a serious problem. The present volume is easily the most comprehensive account of Ottoman manu-facturing available and, in some respects, it is a state-of-the-art summary. Its presence, hopefully, will help to move Ottoman economic and industrial history to a higher methodological plane. But, this volume notwithstanding, quite fundamental issues remain unresolved. Take, for example, the fundamental issue of change over time. The relationship of manufacturing during the seventeenth century to that in the eighteenth or the nineteenth centuries is not at all clear. The contributors to this volume have not reached closure on the issue of whether or not Ottoman industry declined. But perhaps this should not be a cause for pessimism since questions concerning the decline of manufacturing in sixteenth century Italy and in eighteenth century India remain a battleground for scholars. So, Middle East specialists are in good company.

The Ottoman/Turkish story of manufacturing should hold considerable interest for historians of other regions. For such inquiring comparativists, here are some of the parameters of the Ottoman experience that seem most relevant. To begin with, the Ottoman regions were and remained sparsely populated. (Some still are today.) Population densities were greatest in the Balkan lands and least in the Arab provinces. These demographic patterns partly reflected the quality of the agricultural base; soil fertility levels overall are not impressive. Moreover, ground water resources and rainfall are slight. Generally, the Balkan lands are more favored and the Arab lands less. Manufacturing, both by hand and, beginning in the 1870s, by machines in factories, seems to have been more common in the more densely populated, better-watered zones. But, notably, Ottoman Damascus and Aleppo each were major, workshop-based industrial centers.

In this volume, we use the term manufacturing in a very broad sense: the production of goods by hand and by machine in homes, workshops, and factories. Machine production arrived late, visible only in the later nineteenth century. Thus, most of the volume focuses on manufacturing that was done by hand and intended for sale or, in the case of state-sponsored activities, the use, of others, in local and distant domestic markets and in the international market as well.

International rivalry—Indian, Persian/Iranian, Polish, German, French, English—is a familiar part of Ottoman manufacturing history. In addition to facing competition from other Ottoman producers, Ottoman manufacturers in earlier times, until ca. 1750, competed primarily with those further east, especially India and Persia/Iran. From a global perspective, Ottoman (together with New World) producers were among the first to experience intense European competition. Traces of this rivalry from the West are evident in the sixteenth century when European merchants disrupted supplies of raw and semiprocessed goods to Ottoman manufacturers. But head-to-head competition, in the sense of European producers selling large quantities of goods as a substitute for Ottoman-made products, began only in the later eighteenth century.

If they were familiar with international competition, Ottoman producers also were accustomed to working in the presence of a comparatively powerful state. When compared to states in most other areas of the world, the Ottoman state was impressively strong throughout the period.

It also seems relevant to point out that long distance trading networks in the Ottoman lands were disrupted by two events of global importance, temporally quite separate from one another. These were, first, the Portuguese and Columbian voyages of discovery, culminating in successes in 1488 and 1492; and, second, coming almost four centuries later, the development of steamships and the opening of the Suez Canal. The impact of these events on the Ottoman/Middle Eastern manufacturing sector of the respective periods surely holds much for fruitful comparative analysis with, say, the experiences of East Asia and India.

Here, in sum, is the general context within which Ottoman manufacturing evolved over the centuries: it functioned in a slightly settled, agriculturally marginal zone, at an economically sensitive international crossroads, governed by a powerful state.

In the post-Ottoman twentieth century, the various heirs of the Ottoman state actively have been involved in the industrial development of the Balkan, Turkish, and Arab regions. For much of this period, each state respectively sought to play a leading role in directing the economy and each typically focused on import substitution policies. More recently, the successor regimes in Turkey, Egypt, and Syria have turned to the international export market, even to the point of sometimes establishing special export manufacturing zones. The first two states concomitantly have moved to de-emphasize the governmental in favor of the private sector. Surely the story of Ottoman/Turkish manufacturing has relevance when considering the historical and contemporary fate of industry in China, Japan, the Indian subcontinent, and Latin America.

From a different perspective, the activities of Ottoman manufacturers are of considerable importance for the history of European manufacturing as well. The Middle East, for centuries during the medieval and early modern periods, provided Western manufacturers with their largest extraregional export markets, generating capital accumulation for subsequent development in Europe. At certain junctures in the early nineteenth century, moreover, the Ottoman market played a crucial role in the evolution of the English textile industry. Also, the patterns and successes of Ottoman (and earlier) Middle Eastern manufacturers led to changed patterns of production in both eastern and western Europe.

Broadly speaking, manufacturers in the Ottoman Empire and Europe often worked in intimately integrated and interwoven production networks. Manufacturers in both regions not only competed, borrowed, and copied from one another, but they also provided the other with semi-processed materials for finishing. In this view, nineteenth-century Ottoman imports of European, factory-made, yarns and dyestuffs were a continuation of the long-standing relationship between the two manufacturing economies. Two significant changes, however, had taken place. First, the volume of the exchanges had amplified considerably. Second, the previous prevailing rough parity had given way to Western manufacturing superiority. As one commentator, Jonathan Prude, eloquently put it: Ottoman manufacturing in the nineteenth century evolved within an iron cage of European industrialization. The intimacies and longevities in this European-Ottoman manufacturing relationship remain inadequately acknowledged in the historiographies of both regions.

At times, the four authors, because of the source materials that have shaped and sometimes skewed our view of the Ottoman/Turkish industrial economy, differ in their selection and treatment of themes. Abundant documentation led Faroqhi, for example, to discuss slave labor in manufacturing at considerable length, offering fascinating details on the subject. But her own contribution and the previous work of other scholars on the subject make it clear that the use of slaves for economic purposes was unimportant in the Ottoman (and Islamic) world; it was present on very rare occasions and in quite limited numbers. More generally, differences among the four authors often derive from the data bases they used in preparing their contributions. For the period before ca. 1800, there are relatively few alternatives to Ottoman state records as a source of information. In a profound manner, the nature of the data base has shaped the nature of the historical inquiry. Because they are compelled to rely so heavily on official state documents, both Faroqhi and Genç tend to see the world from the state's perspective and they place the state rather close to the center of things. Genç, who researches in the Ottoman dark ages of the eighteenth century, labors under the greatest burden, for the sources of that era usually are purely fiscal in nature and often discontinuous. Thus, his sources inherently are difficult to use for analyses over relatively long periods of time. Despite this, he presents a coherent picture of change during the period; but, it is from a state-centered perspective.

Quataert and Keyder, dealing with the post-1800 world, have access to a vastly greater variety of source materials. Ottoman/Turkish state sources, for their part, become almost unmanageably abundant. In addition, there is a rich host of other materials—including European consular reports, newspapers, and a truly voluminous literature generated by private individuals and, later, corporations. Both had many different kinds of sources at their disposal and more materials on the nonstate factors affecting the manufacturing sector. They tend to offer a more balanced picture of manufacturing activities, both those within and outside the purview of the state. The actual relative importance of the state in manufacturing, moreover, did decline during the nineteenth century, when compared to the earlier periods. Then, during the Turkish republican era, when state economic enterprises became the order of the day, the relative role of the government seems to have expanded again.

Generally, the richness of data on state economic activities often meant that Ottoman historians focused on these efforts, to the exclusion of the nonstate sector. Hence, there has been great stress on government workshops and factories and on production for the imperial palace. In this volume, both Faroqhi and Genç devote considerable space to the state role in controlling artisans. Faroqhi, for her part, explicitly argues against overemphasizing the role of the state in the economy and in manufacturing. But, her contribution, which is based on official documents, mainly mirrors governmental concerns and priorities. Genç's attention to state manufactories also derives from his conviction that state policies in fact did play the crucial role. Ultimately, he argues, the Ottoman government's actions harmed industry and choked off positive developments that had been occurring. Although, as he demonstrates, the state controlled only ten percent of the economy, he justifies his emphasis by comparing that control to a ten percent share in the stockholdings of a modern corporation, which is a participation sufficient to vitally influence the affairs of the enterprise. This focus on state enterprises does pose difficulties. For example, one commentator questioned how Genç could devote a lengthy discussion to fifty looms in an Ottoman state manufacturing enterprise at a time when the textile industry of Lyon held 10 to 17,000 looms![4] Stress upon the state in the economy reflects the presence of strong historiographical traditions rather than actually significant state economic activities.[5] We need to be more cautious when using official sources of information: here, clearly, we see that although the state did play an important role in pre-1800 manufacturing, its importance has been overstated.

The four contributions collectively go far in de-emphasizing the role of the European economy in the evolution of Ottoman/Turkish manufacturing. Faroqhi argues that, in the sixteenth and seventeenth centuries, contact with Europe was too superficial to substantially affect more than a few specific industries. Looking in the countryside for manufacturing activities, she finds vast networks operating, unaffected by Europe. In the manufacturing history of later periods, international forces are given due weight but the discussions focus on the workings of Ottoman manufacturing itself. Thus, Genç places foreign wars at the center of the late eighteenth century economic crisis but centers his attention on internal dynamics. Both Quataert and Keyder take the international economy as a factor of given significance but also prefer to stress the interactions and developments within the Ottoman world.

The question of markets for Ottoman manufactured goods is closely connected to that of Western influence. Here, the three Ottoman specialists—Faroqhi, Genç, and Quataert—give considerable attention to domestic demand, thus de-emphasizing the international export market that long has held the center of scholarly attention. Instead, they seem to argue that, throughout Ottoman history, the domestic market was the crucial variable in determining the well-being of the manufacturing sector. Here, as in their general treatment of the role of the West, they place internal dynamics closer to the center of the explanation for the evolution of the Ottoman economy. The Ottoman economy is their subject of inquiry and not the impact of the West on that economy.

Market questions, in turn, directly related to those concerning capital accumulation: Genç sees the limited nature of export markets as seriously detrimental to capital accumulation during the eighteenth century. But, with the rise of state-imposed cash taxes, peasants made more manu-factured goods for sale. Both peasants and merchants, he argues, were benefitting. Late in the century, however, these promising trends ended, as a fiscally strapped state confiscated the inheritances of the rich. Although the export market rose late in the nineteenth century, significant amounts of investment capital were not forthcoming. Keyder, for his part, holds that the absence of sufficient private capital drove the state into the role of manufacturing entrepreneur.

The spatial patterns of manufacturing, that is, the urban or rural location of work, and whether it was in homes, workshops, or factories emerged as a primary focus of discussion. Rural manufacturing received considerable attention, overcoming a bias in the sources that favors the more visible urban-based production processes. Faroqhi, working with very sparse materials, outlines sixteenth- and seventeenth-century networks of rural manufacturing in several regions. Some of these networks continued for centuries and their story forms part of Quataert's account of manufacturing in the nineteenth century. Genç shows how artisans responded to increasing state pressure by moving to small production centers in rural areas and to more remote neighborhoods in the capital city of İstanbul. In these remoter rural and urban locations, they sought, with some success, to escape the eye and (tax) arm of the state.

All of the authors focus, in varying ways, on the connections between agriculture and industry, the vital impact of the one sector upon the other and the need to study both to understand each. But many details are lacking. We can surmise but cannot establish that households moved in and out of market manufacturing. The significance of changes in the relative weights of urban-rural, workshop-household production remain unclear. In U.S. manufacturing, the shift of households into market-oriented manufacturing is seen as a threshold event but the timing of this transition and its importance in Ottoman history is unknown.[6]

The emergence of mechanized factories late in the Ottoman period and the rise of large-scale state economic enterprises during the era of the Turkish republic are treated and given their proper weight. And yet, as the authors indicate, small manufacturing enterprises have remained important, down to the present day. In sum, the four contributors present small workshops and households as more central to the story of Ottoman/Turkish manufacturing than factories. Vibrant manufacturing in the absence of big factories was the norm; big factories were not seen as a necessary condition for successful industrial production. These findings in Ottoman Middle Eastern history thus form part of the broad-based consensus that has emerged among historians of manufacturing in other regions of the world over the long term. Overall, most historians now agree that small-scale production has been the normal locus of manufacturing. Factories have been the exception, appearing only briefly and belatedly on the historical scene. Since the 1970s, moreover, manufacturing is moving out of factories. Recognition of this so-called second industrial divide generally has rekindled appreciation of the role of home production, small workshops, and putting-out networks.

> [After] the initial boom of mechanization, the most advanced kind of capitalism reverted to eclecticism, to an indivisibility of interests so to speak, as if the characteristic advantage of standing at the commanding heights of the economy...consisted precisely of *not* having to confine oneself to a single choice, of being able, as today's businessman would put it, to keep one's options open.[7]

Issues of Ottoman/Turkish rural and urban, home and factory, production fold into those concerning the mobilization of labor. The characteristic low population densities complicated the problem of finding sufficient workers for the private sector as well as for the state. In such a context, large scale projects were not impossible, but they did require exceptional efforts to mobilize the necessary labor. The state, for its part, often resorted to coercion, in times of both peace and war. Faroqhi, for example, describes how the state overcame labor shortages and attracted miners by offering them a combination of tax relief and wage work. Such practices reverberated down through Ottoman history and, centuries later, we find the state using the same devices to recruit labor in the Zonguldak coal fields. The İstanbul regime, more generally, reached into every area of society for the scarce workers. It sometimes employed tribal members to spin yarn and staff its centralized workshops in provincial regions while, on other occasions in the nineteenth century, it worked through Christian Church authorities to recruit orphans for one of its İstanbul textile factories.

In regards to labor recruitment in the private sector under conditions of scarcity, the sources are nearly always silent for the pre-1800 era. Labor shortages surely exerted upward pressure on wages and, in particular competitive situations, prompted entrepreneurs to look to rural putting-out networks for workers. Late in the Ottoman period, in the nineteenth century, private entrepreneurs who established factories resorted to a number of stratagems to solve the labor problem. Many built their mills in urban centers to be close to the labor sources; this was a great advantage enjoyed by the İstanbul mills. Other urban mill owners erected dormitories near factories to house the female workers that they recruited from the countryside. But when, in order to be near the raw material sources, they built mills away from urban centers, the entrepreneurs used other devices. Take, for example, the cotton spinning and weaving mills that private owners built on the nearly uninhabited Adana plain of southeastern Anatolia during the late nineteenth century. There, with the help of labor contractors, the mill owners recruited a waged workforce of several thousands, sometimes providing them with company kitchens and other amenities.

The guild-like organizations (*esnaf*) of the Ottoman world certainly aided both the state and the private sector in solving the problem of labor shortages in many urban areas. But their prevalence and actual economic significance remains unclear. Urban-based, visible and, particularly in İstanbul, important to the state, they are the frequent focus of Ottomanists' attentions who, once again, are depending on official records for their information. Our enhanced appreciation of rural manufacturing should affect our assessment of the importance of these organizations. It remains an open question whether or not such craft organizations—in whatever manner they actually were organized—provided the majority of even urban-based industrial production before the nineteenth century.

Changes in the structure and nature of the *esnaf* guilds remains similarly uncertain although certain continuities appear evident during the long eighteenth century, until 1820. During this time, for example, the richest artisans received wages that were four to seven times greater than those of the poorest. These differentials hardly suggest egalitarian labor structures. Thereafter, in any event, craft guilds declined and, by ca. 1850, they had disappeared in many (but not all) Ottoman towns and cities. Overall, the authors trace the declining importance of captive labor and of these *esnaf* organizations and chronicle the rising significance of free labor. By the end of the nineteenth century, corvée labor occasionally appears to help build a railroad; but, in general, the Ottoman manufacturing workforce contracted freely in the labor market.

Female and child workers played a prominent role in manufacturing and had been present throughout the entire Ottoman period. They certainly were more visible in the later centuries but this might derive from the more detailed sources available. Females typically were excluded from guilds, but routinely were present as laborers in many government operations, including its workshops and its tribal networks. And they regularly labored in the private sector (outside of the guild membership), working not only in homes, but also in workshops and factories as well. There is the possibility that waged female labor outside of the home became more common in the nineteenth century, in those industries producing for the export market and/or under foreign control.

NOTES

1. The invited discussants were: A. Bagchi (India); N.K. Chaudhuri (India); F. Perlin (India); D. Sella (Italy); C. Poni (Italy); J. Prude (U.S.); F. Zapata (Mexico); A. Feuerwerker (China).

2. Comments by Feuerwerker and Bagchi.

3. For an interesting discussion of these issues in the broader context of Ottoman history, see Abou El-Haj (1991) and the "Introduction" in Quataert (1993a).

4. Comment by Carlo Poni.

5. Comment by Frank Perlin.

6. Comments by Jonathan Prude.

7. Braudel (1982), 381.

PUBLISHED REFERENCES CITED

Rifaat Ali Abou El-Haj
   1991   *The Formation of the Modern State*. Albany, New York.

Fernand Braudel
   1982   *Civilization and Capitalism, 15th–18th Century*, II, *The Wheels of Commerce*. New York.

Donald Quataert
   1993a   *Workers, Peasants and Economic Change in the Ottoman Empire, 1730–1914*. İstanbul.

2

Labor Recruitment and Control in the Ottoman Empire (Sixteenth and Seventeenth Centuries)

Suraiya Faroqhi

This article focuses on the manner in which craftsmen—and in certain special instances craftswomen—were mobilized to participate in production processes too large for the ordinary market and guild to handle. It is probable that, throughout, this paper gives state activities more weight than they deserve. On the surface, it appears that the sixteenth- and seventeenth-century Ottoman state was the major mobilizer of craft labor in Ottoman society. Putting-out merchants, however, may have been underestimated because they left few traces in the primary sources. Absence of documentation is not because they were insignificant, but because written material produced by people outside the state bureaucracy has rarely survived.

Recent research has shown that the Ottoman Empire was not exclusively an agrarian-based military state, which exploited its strategic location controlling the principal trade routes between South Asia and Europe. Ottoman craft industries found a market not only within the

Empire's frontiers but also abroad. In the late fifteenth century, cotton, silk, and angora textiles from Anatolia were exported to the lands north of the Black Sea, while the products of a flourishing leather manufacture are recorded in the price registers of the time.[1] In the late sixteenth century, Ankara mohair cloth found customers in Venice, Poland, and even England, while Ottoman-style leather manufacture established markets in Hungary, and later leathers made in the 'Hungarian' style became popular in France.[2] Copper utensils were not only an item of everyday consumption, but highly decorated examples of this craft were produced for a well-to-do clientele. On the southern shores of the Mediterranean, Tunis had formed part of the Ottoman Empire since 1574. In this city, local craftsmen also worked for a wider market. Into the nineteenth century, Tunisian artisans manufactured red woolen caps, marketed on a large scale throughout North Africa, and also in İstanbul and Anatolia.[3] Even during the eighteenth century, a period that earlier historians regarded as a time of unmitigated decline and that recently has become the subject of some revisionist historiography, there was an appreciable manufacture of textiles for export.[4] Indian cotton fabrics, which had become very popular both in Europe and in the Ottoman Empire from the seventeenth century onward, were copied sucessfully in Eastern Anatolia and the Aleppo region, and as *indiennes* constituted an appreciable item of eighteenth-century French trade. New branches of pre-industrial Ottoman manufactures are constantly being discovered, as a growing number of monographs has put the Ottoman Empire on the map as a significant artisanal producer, mainly of textiles, but also of weapons, copper vessels, and leather goods.

However, raw material procurement, conditions of internal and external trade, and the role of the Ottoman state have attracted much more attention than the producers themselves. This lack of interest can be explained in part by the macroeconomic orientation of many historians who have studied Ottoman manufacturing, and the orientation of our primary sources has reinforced this bias. The Ottoman officials responsible for drawing up the texts that constitute our primary sources were particularly concerned with raw material supplies—the latter formed the basis of production, and without craft production, a whole array of trade-related dues would have been impossible to collect. For the same reason, commercial conditions are reflected in the Ottoman fiscal and political records: foreign merchants had to be prevented from exporting goods that the administration intended to reserve for local producers or, more frequently, for its own use.[5] The stratagems by which merchants tried to avoid customs duties needed to be foiled, while the supply of woolens, cottons, and boots for the army occasioned extensive record-keeping and correspondence.[6] Lastly, practically all documents relating to craft production were produced in the central and provincial administrations. This means that we know quite a few things about matters in which the government intervened, and almost nothing about those which remained outside the administration's purview.

The Ottoman Empire of the classical age resembled both early modern Europe and other agrarian societies with a high level of state organization. In all these societies, trade was better documented than production, and within the manufacturing sphere, conditions under which fixed and moving capital were deployed are more easily studied than the recruitment, remuneration, and control of labor.[7] As a result the present paper consists of a series of puzzles, with attempts at solution which may or may not be convincing.

MOBILIZING LABOR

The vast majority of people were peasants, working family holdings, even though after the population growth of the sixteenth century, quite a few of these farms may have been too small to support a family without intensified production techniques or by employment in manufacturing.[8] Widespread household production and, in many areas, low population densities made it difficult to mobilize labor by purely economic means. In its own projects, the Ottoman state rarely relied on economic incentives. Paying a wage that would have induced craftsmen to quit other employment in favor of work in the Arsenal or a publicly sponsored construction site would have meant major cash expenditures. But cash was chronically in short supply. Similar to most other early modern states the Ottoman Treasury had trouble inducing tax-payers to pay cash, and what little was available was primarily spent on soldiers and war material. As a result, the Ottoman state relied extensively on drafted labor, which was either paid below market rates or not paid at all.[9]

We do not know what the draftees thought of this manner of securing their labor. Within the Ottoman ruling group, the problematic aspects of prestations demanded from the community were discussed, often in the terms of religious law. But these discussions only related to public construction in peacetime, and not to the more burdensome war effort. A pious foundation was not considered to bring the founder religious merit unless the materials, labor, etc., which went into the establishment, were his legitimate property, that is a fair market price had been paid for them. Therefore, sultans establishing a major foundation at least needed to make certain gestures calculated to convince religious scholars and public officials that they had made an effort in this direction.[10] When founding the Süleymaniye mosque complex, Süleyman the Law-giver certainly attempted to make sure that building materials acquired from private persons were properly paid for. Yet Ottoman historians sometimes mention that a certain construction project gave rise to discontent. But even these latter texts do not usually deal with the grievances of poorly paid artisans, but with concerns closer to the minds of the authors and their social equals, such as the forcible relocation of town quarters or the shabby treatment meted out to architects and building administrators.[11] Ömer Lütfi Barkan, to whom we owe a pathbreaking study of the organization of an Ottoman construction site, has concluded that craftsmen and laborers resented being drafted for unpaid labor on fortifications, but did not much object to working on the Süleymaniye site or similar enterprises, where at least they were paid a wage and allowed leave on religious holidays.[12] But this evaluation seems overly optimistic. It assumes that the craftsmen left no families behind, were unable to find better paying employment in their home towns, and traveled in relative comfort. It is difficult to assume that all or even any of these conditions prevailed.

One formula that often has been used to make sense out of the frequent mobilization of Ottoman tax-payers is the characterization of the Empire as a perfect war machine. This formula, which goes back to European observers of the sixteenth century, was taken up by Ömer Lütfi Barkan in his early studies on Ottoman population and rural settlement. Here the political context in which he was writing is of some significance.[13] During World War II, Turkey remained neutral; but its army mobilized for war, an effort that had very negative consequences for an already poor standard of living. 'Military preparedness' and 'willingness to sacrifice' therefore became key items of current official ideology, and by exalting readiness for war as a basic ancestral virtue, the historian was making his own contribution to the war effort. Moreover Barkan, though his perspective on other matters gradually changed in the course of the 1960s and 1970s, never revised his notion of the Ottoman state as a benevolent entity, for the expansion and preservation of which no sacrifice was deemed too great. Nor was there any discussion partner available whose objections might have led him to rethink his position; for the section of Turkish radical intellectuals, with whom he engaged in something like a dialogue during the late sixties and early seventies, had their own reasons for exalting the virtues of a strong and centralized state. Even so, the motif of the 'warfare state' gradually faded out of Ottomanist historiography, while internal policies as a means of securing cohesion loomed larger. In the political context of the last thirty years, 'campaigns and victories' were no longer considered proper subjects for self-congratulation; and so, scholarly concern for the Ottoman state as a mobilizer of labor also declined in consequence.[14]

On a more scholarly level, the notion of the Ottoman Empire as the 'perfect war machine' also has been quietly discredited. This is due to the intensive research on early modern European states, ongoing since the end of World War II, which has shown that most states of the time, with France a particularly well-researched example, mobilized all resources and ruined their peasant populations in an effort to win long and costly wars.[15] In addition, a new focus on provincial history has made scholars aware of the fact that while most provinces were profoundly affected by war-related tax demands, sixteenth- or seventeenth-century wars were not *total wars* in the post-1789 meaning of that term. A few major campaigns apart, the craft and commercial activities of the Empire's cities were not completely interrupted or restructured due to war-time demands. Cairo's trade in coffee and Indian fabrics prospered in the late seventeenth century, uninterrupted by the very destructive and disruptive war of 1683–1699.[16] Thus, most historians of the Ottoman Empire probably would agree that like their neighbors, the Empire's rulers regarded the preparation and conduct of war as their major activities. Perhaps the sixteenth to seventeenth-century Ottoman Empire was somewhat more efficient than its European neighbors in organizing campaigns on land, although, given the lack of appropriate statistics, this is difficult to determine. But given its very sedentary, courtly, and urban culture, it seems scarcely reasonable to describe the Ottoman state as an 'army on the march' or a 'perfect war machine'.[17]

Even if sixteenth- or seventeenth-century wars did not involve a total restructuring of manufactures to expedite the production of war material, craft activities did not remain unaffected. Genç has suggested that the Ottoman Empire's eighteenth-century prosperity (ca. 1700–1770) was cut off by its involvement in a series of costly wars.[18] Since the Ottoman government paid low prices for the war-related deliveries that it demanded, and often refused to pay at all, business suffered. Moreover, he argues, efficient enterprises were affected most seriously, as the administration tended to demand more from effective producers than from

their smaller and poorer competitors. Thus, war pushed down the Ottoman manufacturing sector as a whole to a level of universal mediocrity.
This explanation appears convincing for the eighteenth century, but poses
a major problem for the periods before, particularly the sixteenth and
seventeenth centuries. Why didn't earlier wars generate similarly
destructive crises? But this objection is less serious than that might appear
at first sight, as from the late sixteenth century onward, wars, in fact, did
contribute toward economic crisis. The devaluation of the mid-1580s
coincided with the final years of a protracted war with Iran, while the
difficulties of the subsequent years can be linked with protracted and
indecisive warfare against the Habsburgs, also known as the Long War
(1593–1606). The war of 1683–1699 had dire consequences for economic
life, as the central government cut all expenditures not related to the war
and allowed the security of the roads to deteriorate.[19] Even in this period,
there is no evidence of the kind of war-related boom that has become
familiar to historians of capitalist countries. Nor, at present do we have
any evidence for post-war 'reconversion' crises. As a working hypothesis,
we can assume that Ottoman manufacturing, at least where the sixteenth
to seventeenth centuries were concerned, prospered in times of peace and
contracted in wartime.

The economic role of the Ottoman state involves the (often coerced)
mobilization of craft labor. In this sense, the Ottoman administration can
be allotted a place in Braudel's model of early modern manufacturing,
which distinguishes among isolated craftsmen, artisans whose activities are
controlled and coordinated by merchants, and centralized manufactories
and factories in the narrow sense of the term; the latter are irrelevant for
our purposes.[20] We normally regard Ottoman society as a society whose
manufactured goods were produced by independent artisans, with
putting-out merchants and large-scale manufactories as the exceptions that
prove the rule. But if we include the Ottoman state in our model, we find
that the latter played the role which putting-out merchants played in other
economies, coordinating different stages of manufacturing and mobilizing
labor, albeit by political rather than by economic pressures. Moreover, the
Ottoman state was only marginally concerned with profits, its central
concern being the provisioning of the army, navy, and court.[21] In addition,
the state's activity also obeyed a different time table than that of
putting-out merchants. The latter invested when trade prospered, and
withdrew their funds when markets contracted due to wars, epidemics, or
famines. For the Ottoman state, by contrast, the key variables were peace
and war; in times of war, a much larger section of manufacturing was

forcibly coordinated than in times of peace. War and peace, however, were decided primarily by political, not economic criteria, and this fact probably offset the advantages of scale, which increasing coordination would normally have brought in its wake for manufacturing.

If we were dealing with producers dependent on putting-out merchants, it would be appropriate to group them according to the payment and/or debt links between producers and merchants. In the sixteenth- and seventeenth-century Ottoman source materials, however, debt links are mentioned but rarely. Differentiation according to the dominant mode of payment is not very meaningful either, since many services and deliveries were demanded in lieu of taxes, and hence not paid at all. On the other hand, given the significance of non-economic coercion, I would suggest a taxonomy that takes the manner and degree of coercion into account. Slavery was the most drastic form of coercion, but in the manufacturing sector it was a rare occurrence. Services that demanded that craftsmen move themselves and their workshops to distant locations were surely disruptive to the people affected, even if they were exceptionally well paid. Less disruptive were services that could be rendered in the artisans' own shops. In both cases, we need to distinguish between services the state paid for, albeit at rates below those applied in the market, and demands for unpaid goods and services. Ottoman mining depended on very complex arrangements, and therefore will be treated in a separate section. The money payments that the central administration demanded when the prestation of goods or services were deemed inconvenient is a special case. Whether such payments were more or less disruptive to the craftsmen than deliveries in kind depended on the individual situation, and cannot be determined in an overall fashion. Candidate janissaries constituted another special case of bound labor in manufacturing; soldiers were employed as unpaid and unskilled laborers, and their productive work formed part of their military apprenticeship. Ottoman craftsmen, though technically free men, were subjected by the Ottoman state, at least in certain branches of manufacturing, to varied demands on their time and resources, and it makes sense to regard them as coerced labor for at least part of their active lives.

SLAVERY

The first of the riddles confronting the Ottoman economic historian concerns the silk manufacture of late fifteenth- and early sixteenth-century Bursa—the earliest Ottoman manufacture that is well enough documented for systematic study. In addition to guildmasters with their apprentices and hired laborers who formed the mainstay of production in most Ottoman cities, we encounter a significant number of slave workmen who were employed as weavers and as assistants to merchants.[22] After manumission these slaves sometimes became masters or merchants in their turn.

On the work done by Bursa slave weavers we possess some information due to the institution of *mükâtebe*. This term refers to a contract between master and slave, one recognized by Islamic law and sometimes recorded in the kadi's registers. By this contract the master promised to release the slave after the latter had fulfilled a certain condition, which, in Bursa, quite often was the manufacture of a quantity of silk fabric. Once the agreement had been entered into before witnesses, the master unilaterally could not revoke it. The registers, however, occasionally record slaves declaring themselves unable to fulfil the contract, and thus falling back into unconditional slavery. In the absence of further information, it is impossible to say what kind of pressures slaves may have been subjected to before they made such a declaration.

Nor do we know anything about the manner in which slave weavers were trained. In a listing concerning *mükâtebe* contracts recorded in the 1480s and 1490s, we find a sizeable number of Bosnians, both men and women. Whether these people had learned the sophisticated techniques of manufacturing embroidered velvet or silk gauze in Bosnia, or had been trained in Bursa, remains an open question. But it would seem that certain manufacturers thought it more advantageous to buy trained slaves and emancipate them after they had woven a certain quantity of cloth, than to employ hired laborers; after freeing a slave weaver, they would purchase a new one and enter into another *mükâtebe* agreement.[23] It is possible that certain slave dealers had their slaves trained as silk and brocade weavers to enhance marketability. Such special training for slaves has not so far been documented in the case of weavers, but has often been recorded with respect to young women, who were taught to sing and dance.[24]

Some textile-manufacturing slaves apparently were in business on their own account, for the contracts sometimes specify that the fabrics were to be manufactured in the slave's own workshop. Nor were all inhabitants of Bursa who owned looms necessarily masters occupied full-time in weaving. Looms suitable for the manufacture of highly decorated brocades and velvets were quite expensive. At a time when real estate located in the city changed hands for a few thousand *akçe*, two looms for the manufacture of decorated velvet were sold for six thousand *akçe*.[25] Wealthy people without any direct experience of silk weaving might therefore acquire looms as an investment, and perhaps train slaves to operate this equipment. In certain cases, slave owners set up their emancipated slaves in business by donating or bequeathing them a loom. In October 1485, an owner of three slaves and three looms for the manufacture of figured velvet recorded having taken care of two Russians and one Bosnian in this fashion.[26]

Arrangements of this kind now and then could probably be found in other cities of Anatolia and the Balkans as well. But the most remarkable fact about Bursa was the high proportion of slaves and freedmen (tied to their former owners in a client relationship). It has been estimated that in the late fifteenth and early sixteenth centuries, about fifteen percent of the Bursa population were former slaves. The sources do not provide any information on the people whose fathers or mothers had been slaves, but the number of Bursalıs with an immediate experience of slavery must have been higher still. According to a more debatable estimate, as many as twenty- to twenty-five percent of all Bursa inhabitants may have been slaves.[27] Moreover the kadi registers of the late fifteenth and early sixteenth centuries frequently mention ex-slaves as merchants and craftsmen. In late fifteenth- and early sixteenth-century Bursa, slaves were not simply prestige possessions of the wealthy and powerful, but played a significant role in productive work.

This rather unique situation calls for some explanation. Research done on other Ottoman cities on the basis of kadi registers is now quite plentiful, and none of the monographs on Ankara, Konya, Kayseri, Mardin, or Aleppo say very much on the role of slaves in social and economic life.[28] Slavery in Bursa likely was much more economically significant than elsewhere. İstanbul with its high concentration of officials, who were often wealthy and easily acquired slaves, may have contained a larger unfree population; but then İstanbul was not a manufacturing center on a par with Bursa. To explain the high concentration of slaves in Bursa, Halil Sahillioğlu has suggested that an unusually high demand for labor, combined with the availability of liquid wealth, was the root cause for the activity of the local slave market.[29] Even the sultans, when they wished to divest themselves of unwanted slaves, had recourse to the Bursa slave traders.

Surprisingly enough, a recent study of seventeenth-century Bursa, which particularly concerns itself with the structure and social origins of the labor force, makes no mention at all of slaves.[30] This is not, of course,

conclusive evidence of the declining economic and social role of slavery;
Ottoman urban studies do not possess a widely accepted agenda requiring
every urban historian to address the topic of slavery. But the phenomenon
was not as common in the seventeenth century as it had been one or two
hundred years earlier. Slavery may well have become less significant in
Bursa's economic life as the city's commercial radius narrowed, and the
city came to depend less on imported Iranian raw silk and more upon the
local production. Apparently seventeenth-century Bursa was a regional
center producing silk fabrics for the wealthy people of İstanbul, while in
the late 1400s and early 1500s it had been a hub of interregional and
international trade, selling silk fabrics to distant markets. With these links
weakened, there was less money available for the purchase of slaves. But
at the same time, the shift to a regional economy gave a chance to poor
but free people, who now no longer were competing against slave labor.
The growth of local silk-raising and the beginnings of a putting-out
industry provided work for the indigent, who seem to have been slightly
less destitute toward the end of the seventeenth century than they had
been at the beginning.[31] If all this is true, then the decline of Bursa's
international trade links, which probably began with the interruption of
the Iranian silk trade by Sultan Selim I (1512–1520) and was intensified by
European competition for raw silk during the second half of the sixteenth
century, also led to a dramatic change in the composition of the city's
working population.

Apart from Bursa, the employment of slaves by private masters is
also documented for Algiers. However, in the absence of court registers,
even a semblance of quantification is impossible. Some data can be
gleaned from Spanish and Roman inquisition accounts.[32] But these
documents concern only people who, after having lived as Muslim
converts for varying periods, returned to Spain or Italy either voluntarily or
because they had been captured. It appears that craftsmen were much in
demand in Algiers and Tunis, particularly gunsmiths and shipbuilders. To
mention a few examples: Mateo Castellano from Teneriffa was a specialist
in repairing ships and as Ossaim (Husayn) he continued his trade with the
Algerian fleet, later becoming a ship captain; a carpenter from Mallorca
also rose to the rank of captain, he had converted to Islam on the day that
the twenty-five bench galley that he had constructed was first put to sea at
Algiers.[33] The witnesses who described the fate of these two men had
seen them at the time of their prosperity, but, it is very probable that both
began their Algerian careers as slave craftsmen. Other slave craftsmen
were barbers and surgeons, serving the seamen of the navy, the janissaries

of Algiers and Tunis, and in one instance, the inmates of the governor's palace. Silk weavers, carders, shoemakers, and tailors are also recorded.

A high demand for the services of craftsmen made the ownership of slave artisans very profitable. Returnees often claimed that their masters had refused exchange or ransom when they found their captive to be a skilled artisan.[34] Since the Inquisition frequently imposed monetary penalties, most artisans and commercial employees preferred to say nothing about their North African earnings. But some masters were known to allow their slaves control of appreciable funds, even though, legally speaking, slaves could not own property. In fact, some slaves were able to buy their freedom with money they had earned during slavery. A former soldier to the King of Poland even described how the arrangement worked out in his own case. His master, after recognizing his skill as an armorer, opened a workshop for him on the island of Chios, and allowed his slave to retain a share of the profits.[35]

Very little is known about the slaves belonging to the state (*miri esirler*) who sometimes were employed in different branches of manufacturing. Their numbers apparently remained quite small. In the İstanbul Arsenal, slave craftsmen were employed and easily are recognized in wage account books because they received not wages, but a small sum of money for their food and other needs (*nafaka*).[36]

Servile labor was also encountered on Ottoman public construction projects. When the Süleymaniye mosque and pious foundation complex was built between 1550 and 1557, slaves, who apparently belonged to the Ottoman fisc, performed five percent of all man-hours expended. One might add that the servitors of the Sultan, who were trained in the Palace to serve as high-level military commanders and administrators, sometimes also learned a craft; and those who showed aptitude might develop their skills without jeopardizing their future political and military careers. Thus Mehmed Ağa, later the Chief Architect in charge of the Sultan Ahmed mosque, learned how to make inlaid furniture, and presented the ruler with items he had manufactured with his own hands.[37] But his was an unusual career in many respects, and *devşirme* recruits, while slaves of the Sultan, cannot be regarded as slaves in the ordinary sense of the term.[38]

Both at Bursa and Algiers, slave craftsmen played a prominent role for only a limited period. But the fact that slave artisans did come to be important in certain local economies demonstrates that the Ottoman ruling group of the 'classical period' did not regard slavery as an institution that should remain limited to the domestic sector, a view apparently widespread in the nineteenth century.[39] Moreover slaves were important at the height of Bursa's involvement in international trade, while their role declined in the seventeenth century along with the city's economic importance. This phenomenon can be explained by economic factors. There is no evidence that the Ottoman administration of the sixteenth and seventeenth centuries attempted to abolish or phase out slavery in manufacturing. It liberated only the remote descendants of war captives, settled in villages of serfs tied to the soil and often inherited from pre-Ottoman principalities.[40]

Moving Men Around: Draftees in the Labor Force

The day-to-day functioning of the Ottoman central administration, including the court, the army, and the navy, depended on the services of craftsmen who served by administrative fiat, and who often received wages significantly below the market rate. The forms of coercion varied as did the impact upon the lives of the craftsmen involved. We now will discuss goods and services that craftsmen rendered to the state, first those which demanded temporary relocation of the craftsmen and their shops, then prestations which could be rendered without relocation, money payments in lieu of prestations, and labor in the manufacturing sector performed by military men. In addition to the four categories outlined above, we encounter certain instances in which artisans, though technically free men, were required to move permanently, which means that they generally took their families along with them. Permanent relocation often happened in the wake of war. Among the large number of people settled in İstanbul after the Ottoman conquest, there must have been many artisans, but in their case, the main aim was not to secure the services of craftsmen but more generally to ensure the revival of the city.[41] After the Ottoman conquest of Tabriz in 1514, a thousand artisans, merchants and *ulema* were transferred to İstanbul.[42] Also, after the Ottoman conquest, Egyptian manufacturers of rugs were in demand at the Ottoman court and a number of expert artisans were expected to set up a workshop in İstanbul.[43] The artisans in question probably were required to move to İstanbul on a permanent basis.

Many more people were affected by projects of specific duration, such as military and building campaigns, the number and scope of which resulted in a permanent shortage of trained manpower. To remedy this situation, the kadis of specific localities were ordered to round up the number of men needed, make sure of their qualifications and send them to their place of employment, quite often İstanbul.[44] Upon arrival, measures were taken to prevent their escape. They frequently were lodged together in the same khan that was locked up overnight. Non-Muslim draftees were sometimes required to hand in their poll-tax receipts for the current year. This latter practice, however, is attested only for the eighteenth century.[45]

Craftsmen working on building and other projects sponsored by the Ottoman central administration received an officially determined wage. Probably the local kadi played a role in deciding the amount to be paid. In at least a few instances, artisans demanded more than what was officially conceded. In 1587, masons, stonecutters, and carpenters refused to work for the twelve *akçe* wage the government had allotted and demanded sixteen *akçe* instead.[46] The administration granted this request, probably because the devaluation of the *akçe* in 1584–86 increased prices, causing difficulties for the artisans.[47] But the workers on the Sokollu Mehmet Pasha mosque were not satisfied with the increase. They demanded more money and refused to work unless their demands were met. Presumably at the instigation of Sokollu Mehmet Pasha, who was Grand Vizier at the time of this dispute, the workmen's request was turned down and the government ordered them back to work.

This case is of some interest because it reveals the mechanisms by which the Ottoman government hoped to contain craftmen's demands. Apart from impressing the rebellious artisans by admonishing a number of them in some suitably official place, the government put pressure upon the foremen (*halife*) who held permanent positions (*gedik*). The foremen were responsible for tracking down workmen who left their jobs without permission, in case of negligence, the latter were threatened with loss of their own positions. The foremen had to be present when the government's orders were promulgated and probably were expected to persuade the craftsmen to accept the wages that the Ottoman administration was willing to pay.

We know of certain instances in which these measures did not work. In İstanbul, private demand for construction workers was not limited to the Jewish quarters, and craftsmen 'disappeared' to find private employment. This explains how turnover was reasonably high on a major construction site such as the Süleymaniye.

Little is known about modes of payment. Records were kept for every day, showing the names of the workmen actually in attendance, but we do not know whether they were normally paid by the day, week, or month, and how frequently their pay was in arrears.[48] A panegyric account of the construction of the Sultan Ahmed mosque refers to the Chief Architect paying the workmen with his own hands at the end of the day.[49]

Fully-fledged artisans were accompanied by less-skilled workmen, who were paid one half or slightly less than the masters' wages. We do not know whether these men received their pay directly from the accounting bureau of the relevant construction site, or whether the master craftsmen passed on the money owed to their aides. Some craftsmen took on major jobs against payment of a lump sum. When the Sultan Ahmed mosque was being built at İstanbul in the early seventeenth century, a Greek entrepreneur by the name of Yorgi took on a contract worth 299,132 *akçe*.[50] This was a respectable sum, compared to the 6.9 million *akçe* spent on the sea transport of all the materials needed on the construction site.[51] Other contractors undertook even more substantial contracts; one was worth more than a million *akçe*. Some of these contracts cut across guild limits. The Greek entrepreneur just mentioned had installed glass windows, painted the mosque's main dome and southern half dome prior to its decoration by the *nakkaş*, and put in the entire tile decoration. It is probable that two or three guilds were involved in this operation; but whether Yorgi directly negotiated with them, or relied on the central administration for workmen, remains an open question. Other contracts probably operated within a single guild. The construction accounts of the Sultan Ahmed mosque refer to *götüriciyan* among the stone and marblecutters. Since *götüri* in Ottoman means 'everything, totality', these people, whom the text differentiates from the *gündelikçiyan* (day laborers), must have undertaken sizeable jobs in return for lump sum payments.[52] Whether investment in building contracts was profitable or whether the contractors had been drafted to perform this service, cannot presently be determined.

Sizeable numbers of drafted workmen were employed in the İstanbul Arsenal. Navy galleys and round ships needed frequent replacement. In addition, preparation for war and the aftermath of naval battles required the construction of large numbers of ships in a short time. In the seventeenth century, when the Arsenal was probably less active than it had been in the 1560s or 1570s, this largest manufactory of the Ottoman Empire annually could make up to 130 ships per year.[53] But when naval activity was at a low ebb, as in the early seventeenth century, the Arsenal turned out only a few ships *per annum* and in some years was used for repairs only. These violent ups and downs explain why the Arsenal often must have kept only a limited permanent staff, and relied on drafted labor in periods of peak activity.

Arsenal workers were drafted for the Cretan War, when initial Venetian successes in the Dardanelles area made the need for more ships dramatically clear. Sometimes recruitment was in the hands of the kadis, but the central administration also attempted to speed things up by sending out special officials (*çavuş*) who rounded up the craftsmen and oversaw their transfer to İstanbul.[54] Sometimes the Ottoman administration drafted shipbuilders specialized in the construction of merchantmen. Many of these men came from the Anatolian Black Sea coast, where forests were still ample and agricultural land difficult to find; this area supplied carpenters and augerers. In the seventeenth century, most Arsenal workers were Christians, while at the beginning of the sixteenth century the majority had been Muslims.[55] This change probably had something to do with recruitment patterns. In the 1520s, young soldiers who were candidates for positions as janissaries (*acemi oğlan*) often served in the Arsenal; these people obviously were Muslims. On the other hand, early seventeenth-century janissaries were less frequently a product of the child tribute (*devşirme*) and more often entered the corps as the sons of soldiers. Such people apparently found ways of avoiding service in the Arsenal, while the coastal strip along the Black Sea, where many seventeenth-century Arsenal workmen had been born, possessed a sizeable Christian population.

Wages paid in the mid-seventeenth-century Arsenal were about the same as those of the disgruntled building craftsmen of 1580s mosque projects. In those days, the standard pay had been sixteen *akçe* for masters and eight for workers. In the seventeenth century foremen received twenty *akçe*, master craftsmen ten to sixteen *akçe* and apprentices three to six *akçe*.[56] The value of the *akçe*, however, had not been stable in the meantime. Before 1600, 115 *dirhem* of bread cost one *akçe*. The currency reform of that year brought the official price down to 200 *dirhem/akçe*; but the price soon increased to 150 in 1640, when another currency reform again lowered the price to 200. It is very probable that the price of bread soon went up again, and particularly the lower-paid workmen must have had difficulty making ends meet. At a bread price of 200, sixteen *akçe* bought 9.9 kg of bread.[57] If we assume that an ordinary craftsman's family consumed about 5 kg bread a day, in good years fifty percent of the breadwinner's earnings had to be paid out for bread. Thus the İstanbul masons and carpenters who had been drafted for work on official projects received wages that by the standards of pre-industrial Europe can be considered as normal, although they certainly did not permit a comfortable standard of living. It was usual enough in late eighteenth-century Paris for artisans to spend forty to sixty percent of their wages on bread. A mason's family living in Berlin about 1800 spent forty-four percent of its earnings on this basic commodity.[58]

If it is true that craftsmen were drafted because they would not have volunteered for the central administration's projects, wages in the open market should have been higher. The register of administratively determined prices promulgated in 1640, in fact, does fix the wages of İstanbul carpenters at twenty to twenty-five *akçe* per day; those artisans thus carried home the equivalent of 12.4 to 15.5 kg of bread.[59] A family of five, consuming 5 kg bread a day, would have spent thirty-two to forty percent of its earnings on bread. By the standards of the time, this constituted a very reasonable wage. Presumably İstanbul wages were tolerable because of brisk demand for skilled labor; unskilled workers and servants continued to live in poverty.

Thus, we can envisage the financial sacrifice demanded of a skilled carpenter or mason who was unable to avoid the minions of the local kadi or recruiting *çavuş* It is much more difficult to measure the sacrifices of the craftsmen who were recruited at the beginning of each campaign to accompany the armies and supply the soldiers with the necessary goods and services (*orducu*). In this case, the artisan did have to move only two times, as happened to the employees of public construction sites or the Arsenal, but shared all the risks and discomforts of a lengthy campaign. It is likely that the wages paid such artisans were modest if, indeed, they did not have to serve the soldiers without any pay at all.

There were frequent disputes concerning the manner in which the number of craftsmen needed should be divided up among the different guilds. Certain guilds carried the principal responsibility, while less important guilds were assigned auxiliary services as *yamak*.[60] In small places, arrangements concerning the *orducu* sometimes were made in a public meeting to limit the probability of fraud. After the governor's orders had been promulgated, certain guildsmen might object to the arrangement, particularly if the orders were seen to violate what local people regarded as immemorial custom. If the number of men to be supplied was higher than usual, complaints also ensued; but the chances of simple artisans resisting demands from the central state probably were limited.[61]

A surviving list of İstanbul artisans, called up to participate in a mid-sixteenth century campaign, gives us some idea of the orders of magnitude involved. A total of 133 artisans included bakers and sellers of barley, responsible for preparing the basic nourishment of man and beast.[62] There were tailors, shoemakers, sellers of different types of cloth, and druggists cum spice-sellers. These civilian artisans probably were meant to supplement the work done by the soldiers themselves, provide expert guidance, undertake more complicated repairs, and maybe cater to the more expensive tastes of the officers.

Certain craftsmen were required to help man the navy as oarsmen.[63] This obligation is relevant in the present context, even though rowers were not employed in manufacturing, for this requirement cost İstanbul craftsmen labor and money, and thereby made it more difficult for them to function as productive units. The demand for rowers from İstanbul craftsmen appears for the first time during the Ottoman-Venetian war over Crete, in 1646.[64] At this time the cabaretiers, sellers of millet beer, boatmen, porters, and non-Muslims of the city together were required to supply a total of 337 rowers; ten years later this figure had increased to over two thousand. In 1646 the cabaretiers had to provide the lion's share; this was doubtlessly meant to be a means of penalizing a trade widely regarded as discreditable. However in later years the cabarets of İstanbul were, once again, closed down, and the cabaretiers, who now had to find themselves another means of making a living, were absolved from their responsibilities toward the navy (1671). The consequent demand from the other guildsmen for equal treatment was rejected because their service was regarded as equivalent to the obligation to provide grain for the armies, one which the İstanbul craftsmen were liable to in the same way as other tax-payers.

The İstanbul artisans required to supply oarsmen were apparently selected in a quite pragmatic fashion. Makers and sellers of millet-beer probably got on the lists because their establishments were linked to cabarets. Boatmen and porters already possessed the rowing skills, physical force and endurance galley rowers needed, while the non-Muslims were tacked on when it seemed that the demand for rowers endangered the continuance of transportation services within İstanbul.

It is difficult to decide whether the artisans employed in court workshops, making fine rugs, pottery or illustrated books, should be regarded as coerced labor. Since their work demanded close attention and application, not to be expected from draftees, something must have been done to make the effort worth their while. Yet, the ability of the Sultan to demand his subjects' services at below-market-price remuneration was so clear that it is hard to imagine that all court artisans had taken up service on a purely voluntary basis.[65] The overall level of coordination between different workshops serving the court is a matter of debate that revolves around the meaning of the widespread occurrence of certain decorative motifs in very different branches of court art. Some argue for the existence of a centralized 'designers' office' in which artists drew sketches which other craftsmen then transferred onto brocades, İznik pottery, or inlaid furniture; but others have challenged this interpretation.[66] Designers may well have adopted certain motifs because the latter were in favor with the Sultan or high court officials. Since the Ottoman Palace relied on private manufacturers for most of its fine textiles, there may have been a more centralized system of regulation in those cases where workshops were operated directly by the Palace.

SERVICES PERFORMED IN THE PRODUCERS' OWN SHOPS AND WORKPLACES

Among the goods produced by craftsmen in their native towns, by far the best known are the woolen textiles (*çuha*) produced by Jewish weavers in Salonica, from which janissary uniforms were made. In the fifteenth century, woolen fabrics of medium to better quality often were imported from Italy or indirectly from Flanders. A concern with 'import substitution' apparently prompted Sultan Bayezid II (1481–1512) to allow the immigration of Sephardic Jews, then being driven out of Spain. They were to weave woolen cloth according to specimens delivered to them every year by the Ottoman central administration, for which they received payment according to the (relatively low) prices that the government paid.[67] Certain deliveries also were demanded in lieu of taxes, that is, the craftsmen did not receive any remuneration at all. In order to support themselves, manufacturers also supplied medium-quality cloth to private customers; luxury woolens continued to be imported from Europe.

At the height of their prosperity in the sixteenth and seventeenth centuries, the woolen manufacturers of Salonica had an elaborate division of labor. From 1664 onward, cloth was woven in large halls; these, however, were not integrated enterprises since industrial masters apparently retained their economic independence.[68] Rather, they constituted devices to facilitate control of the quality of the fabric. After weaving, the cloth was sent to the countryside, where abundant streams permitted fulling by water power. Three villages, inhabited by Jewish textile workers, specialized in fulling. It is not known whether these people also eked out livelihoods from agriculture. The cloth was then taken back to Salonica and handed over to the responsible official (*emin*).[69] When the weavers received payment, the *emin* also disbursed the necessary sums of money.

This arrangement could work only if the craftsmen had assured raw material supplies and a market among private customers. To secure the wool, Salonica weavers were given the privilege of purchasing Balkan raw wool before it was offered to other buyers. The private market in woolen fabrics was not protected. Indeed, Ottoman officials generally regarded imports favorably, as a source of increased supply and thus of low prices. Therefore, the growth of the Venetian woolen industry in the second half of the sixteenth century posed a new threat to the Salonica manufacturers, for the Venetians competed for Balkan wool and probably were able to offer better prices.[70] At the same time, the importation of Venetian woolen fabrics, also of medium quality, limited private demand for the Salonica product. After 1600, the growth of the Venetian woolen industry ceased and then turned into a rapid decline.[71] But this provided little relief to the Salonica manufacturers, for Balkan wool continued to be demanded by foreign, particularly French, manufacturers. At the same time, English ships had begun to enter the Mediterranean in full force during the closing decades of the sixteenth century, and pressed their advantage after 1600. For English merchants, the sale of woolen cloth constituted but a secondary business, and they were willing to offer low prices instead of letting the ships travel in ballast on the outgoing voyage. Moreover, domestic demand was contracting due to financial crisis, as the emoluments of Ottoman officials came in irregularly and their purchasing power declined. Fiscal crisis hit the Salonica manufacturers from yet another angle: for the central administration, in an attempt to save cash, stopped paying for the deliveries it demanded and obliged manufacturers to hand over more cloth in lieu of taxes.[72] From the middle of the seventeenth century onward, the industry ceased to be profitable, and became purely an adjunct to the janissary corps. In this rudimentary fashion, it survived until the abolition of the janissaries in 1826.

Economic difficulties were compounded by administrative problems, and the latter were more obvious to contemporaries than the former. The complaints of the Salonica craftsmen rarely deal with foreign competition, and very frequently with officials (*emin*) who demanded bribes, refused to let the weavers move from the congested city into the countryside during a major plague epidemic, or used fraudulent yardsticks.[73] The low quality of the (fairly subordinate) officials responsible for the deliveries, and the pressure they put upon the weavers, were in themselves the outcome of Ottoman fiscal crisis. Many Salonica craftsmen responded by emigration, either to other Macedonian towns or to the other shore of the Aegean Sea, where the growing city of İzmir readily absorbed non-Muslim migrants.[74] Most of this migration was illegal, for even though the weavers were not slaves, they were tied to the city of Salonica by administrative fiat. From the central administration's point of view, the cloth manufacturers were obliged to provide woolen cloth and if the latter moved to other localities, the less than elastic bureaucratic apparatus would have been incapable of satisfying the janissaries' demand.

In exchange, the Salonica cloth manufacturers enjoyed exemption from the ordinary system of law enforcement. Normally, Ottoman subjects who had infringed the law were punished by the governors' men, especially the *subaşı*. However the Salonica weavers were treated as if they were janissaries, and could only be punished by janissary officers.[75] This was probably a substantial privilege, since the appointees of a governor who remained in office for just a short time possessed a reputation for violence and corruption; subjects of the Empire employed all possible ruses to be declared servitors of the state and thereby escape the governors' jurisdictions. In addition, the Salonica cloth manufacturers also enjoyed the coveted privilege of exemption from *avarız-ı divaniye* and *tekâlif-i örfiye*, which were especially burdensome because the amounts to be demanded could not be calculated in advance.[76] Thus, at least on paper, limitations on the craftmen's freedom to move and to produce were counterbalanced by special privileges. Economic conjuncture determined whether the advantages or the disadvantages dominated. In the early sixteenth century, there is little evidence of weavers' discontents, but this may be due only to the limited amount of available documentary evidence. During the seventeenth century, the gradual dispersal of the manufacturing community shows that tax privileges were no longer sufficient to offset the disadvantage of employment in a decaying industry.

In addition to woolen coats, janissary uniforms also consisted of cotton underclothing. Since cotton cloth is easier to weave than woolens, its manufacture remained dispersed throughout the towns and villages of Thessaly and Western Anatolia.[77] At the same time, official demand was much greater since the navy also required large quantities of sailcloth. It is impossible to say whether the weavers were mainly urban craftsmen or villagers for whom weaving constituted an auxiliary occupation. The principal centers of cotton weaving were located in areas where villages and small towns predominated, many weavers probably were part-time agriculturalists. The latter were, in principle, paid for their services. But given the central administration's chronic lack of cash, tax farmers in charge of collecting local dues were often required to advance the money to pay weavers for their services to the central administration. For the tax farmer, requests of this kind constituted a serious liability, since he was then obliged to provide cash at a much earlier time than originally foreseen.[78] Many tax farmers sought to avoid this additional drain upon their resources by absconding or pleading bankruptcy. It is therefore probable that the weavers' pay was often badly in arrears and administrative coercion needed to keep them at work.

We know even less about other services to the Ottoman commissariat, particularly the milling of grain into flour or the baking of ship biscuit (*peksimed*). Hard biscuit was consumed not only by sailors but also by the soldiers whom the Ottoman administration sent to Mecca every year to escort the hajj caravan. It therefore was required in large quantities. Milling probably was mainly undertaken by villagers. In the later sixteenth and the early seventeenth centuries, deliveries of flour figured prominently among the requisitions known as *nüzul* and *sürsat*. *Nüzul* was considered a tax and deliveries demanded under this heading were not remunerated. *Sürsat*, theoretically speaking, was a requirement to sell supplies, and not a tax in the narrow sense of the word. But the central administration retained the right to fix prices, and the latter were often so low that deliveries amounted to confiscation. Moreover *nüzul* and *sürsat* involved transporting the supplies thus requisitioned to fixed collecting points. Given the scarcity and high cost of overland transport, shipping costs must have made the delivery of flour into a source of heavy losses to the villagers.[79]

Sürsat and *nüzul* levies were supervised by the kadis, who acted as the central administration's 'men-on-the-spot' for all kinds of other levies as well. Kadis also received imperial commands to assure supplies of ship biscuit. But to date we do not know how they went about it.[80] Moreover in the middle of the sixteenth century, the Ottoman central administration sometimes extended 'investment credit' to small entrepreneurs such as the iron smelters of Samakov, who otherwise could not expand production.[81] Again the kadis were required to act as middlemen, locally collecting information on the probability of actual deliveries of the pledged iron. In case of default, the kadi had to make good the losses out of his own pocket. Many kadis were placed in a difficult position, since they did not command a police force capable of tracking down absconders. Moreover, as their terms of appointment were too short for them to develop significant social and economic ties to the smelters, the financial risks involved thus were high. Süleyman the Lawgiver's administration responded to the resulting complaints by absolving the kadis from this responsibility and employing contractors instead. The latter took over the distribution of loans and (presumably) retained a share of the money disbursed by the central administration; under these circumstances, making up for losses due to defaulting debtors became an ordinary business expense. State loans to craftsmen, we can surmise, probably were not granted frequently, but we cannot speculate about how often profit-making middlemen were involved.

CAPITAL AND LABOR IN MINING

Arrangements for securing capital and labor needed in the mining of iron and copper, as well as for the extraction of salt, alum, and saltpeter, were extremely complex.[82] Sometimes the central administration relocated skilled miners, and also mobilized local people who retained their farms and mined on a part-time basis. Slave labor was not unknown; to date, however, slave miners have been documented only for the seventeenth-century copper mines of Küre in North-Central Anatolia, where working conditions were particularly bad.[83]

The Ottoman Sultan claimed ownership of all subsoil resources, even though this claim did not, particularly in Rumelia, prevent recognition of subordinate ownership rights vested in mining operators.[84] State officials, however, did not usually directly manage the mines as was normal in the case of the Arsenal, public construction sites and court workshops. Direct management was a last resort, when the operation of a mine proved unprofitable. Otherwise, contractors supplied working capital, farming a mine as they would have farmed the taxes of a town or village. These contractors likely also provided managerial skills, either by personal supervision or by hiring people to do the job. Contractors took over mines for a period of several years; tenures, however, could be prematurely terminated if the central administration received a better offer.

Selling the iron, copper, or alum produced was a matter of survival for the contractor. Without sales, he could not pay the central administration and non-payment could land him in jail; certain taxfarmers were even executed for non-payment of debts.[85] The central administration facilitated disposal by political arrangements, thus, a given mine's product was granted a monopoly for a predetermined region (örü), where it could be sold at monopoly prices. When supply exceeded demand, certain kinds of customers were required to purchase set quantities of mineral at administratively determined prices, and people engaged in transporting a low-demand mineral, such as alum, were paid in kind; saddled with the problem of finding purchasers.[86] Thus the farmers of the more important mines were key figures in mobilizing labor for the

Ottoman central administration. Moreover, they constituted a crucial link between the command economy run by the Ottoman central administration and the everyday market exchanges by which the majority of Ottoman subjects made a living.

We know very little about the technical aspects of Ottoman mines and the skilled foremen, but somewhat more is known about ordinary miners. In many cases, miners possessed small farms and worked the mines on a part-time basis. The Ottoman government's rationale for this arrangement was expressed in 1568–69, in a set of tax regulations dealing with the East Anatolian province of Erzurum.[87] Ottoman officials had tried to employ wageworkers without any ties to agriculture; ultimately it returned to the employment of peasant miners because the area was hilly and infertile. Through mining, the villages could work off their obligations and thereby stay on the land. Thus, the miners of Şebinkarahisar in the province of Erzurum functioned in a manner quite comparable to what is known about disadvantaged areas in seventeenth and eighteenth-century Europe, where peasants unable to make a living due to poor natural or socio-economic conditions eked out a living by rural industry.[88]

But not all miners in sixteenth- and seventeenth-century Anatolia served in the mines merely to work off tax obligations. In the iron mines of Kiğı, also in Erzurum province, miners petitioned the government for higher wages.[89] These wages were derisory, compared with those paid on other public building projects of the period, but prices in the remote villages of Erzurum province were lower than those of more commercially active regions.[90] The fact that the miners went to the trouble and expense of complaining to the administration in İstanbul shows that their pay was of significance to them. In this mountainous and infertile area, miners, to some extent, probably depended on foodstuffs brought in from outside. Normally, this would not have been feasible due to the high price of transportation. But in the case of mining villages, a special situation obtained. Since local people were in charge of transporting the finished product (often cannon balls) to the collecting points of the Ottoman army, roads were available. And, since animals and transportation workers had to return to the mining villages once their work was completed, transportation costs were lessened. The miners may well have paid for part of the food with the money they earned as wages. This in turn would explain why their pay was of vital importance to them.

Concerning the iron mines of Kiğı, we find frequent references to labor shortage. In itself, the custom of drafting laborers indicates that they did not come forward voluntarily.[91] Also, it is clear that not all mines and smelting works were staffed with local people, in whose lives the ironworks had a definite place and who could more or less foresee demands to be made on them. In addition, we find outside laborers sometimes living in nearby settlements, but often brought from some distance. These people were likely to seize every opportunity to avoid extra demands on their labor. Presently it is impossible to say which of these two categories was numerically more significant.

PAYMENTS BY CRAFTSMEN IN PLACE OF SERVICE

The history of labor services in the 'classical age' Ottoman Empire, and their subsequent evolution remains to be written. In the present article, only a few aspects can be touched upon, since most of these services concern agriculture and transportation, not manufacturing. Yet the manufacturing sector, as we have seen, did not remain untouched; and thus we find craftsmen paying dues that constituted an adjunct to labor services, or else the money equivalent of service.

When artisans were sent out to accompany the Ottoman army on campaign, the money they needed to establish their shops was collected from their colleagues who were fortunate enough to stay behind.[92] This arrangement had something in common with the regulations, that endured well into the seventeenth century, financing the services of nomad auxiliaries to the Ottoman armies.[93] These Rumelian nomads, who had lost their tribal organization at an early date, were grouped into military units known as *ocaks*. Each *ocak* sent members to serve in the army, while the remainder supplied tents, horses and weaponry. From the viewpoint of the sixteenth- and seventeenth-century Ottoman administration (if not necessarily the craftsmen themselves), craft guilds functioned in the same manner as *ocaks*, and relieved the finance department from responsibility for a crucial section of the commissariat.

In addition, certain İstanbul craftsmen paid a tax in lieu of serving as rowers in the navy. During the second half of the seventeenth century, the central administration reserved the right to demand the actual performance of this service or a sum of money in its stead. The amount payable varied.[94] This arrangement can be explained by the fact that there were destitute men available, who served on a voluntary basis, or at least the recording officials liked to think of them as volunteers.[95] Money collected from İstanbul craftsmen (*bedel-i kürekçi*) could be used to hire oarsmen from this group, an arrangement which also suited the artisans. However the *bedel-i kürekçi* dues never gained the importance of other payments in lieu of service, such as the tax by which the holders of eighteenth-century tax assignments (*timar*) could be excused from participation in campaigns.

MILITARY MEN IN MANUFACTURING

The Ottoman administration frequently used soldiers as laborers. About forty percent of the labor hours required to build the Süleymaniye mosque complex were performed by candidate janissaries (*acemi oğlan*).[96] The central administration saved money because the soldiers, when not urgently needed in the field, could perform productive labor as an equivalent to their pay. *Acemi oğlan* were poorly remunerated; for their subsistence, the administration paid only one to two *akçe* a day, while unskilled laborers generally received five to seven *akçe*. However the *acemi oğlan* were lodged and clothed, and possibly even fed. From the commanding officers' viewpoint, this arrangement had the additional advantage that discipline problems were lessened, as labor on an officially sponsored project normally entailed close supervision.

Some *acemi oğlan* learned a trade in the course of their service. We find them in the Palace where they worked in the saddlery. They also served in the workshops associated with the janissary commander's office (*Ağa kapısı*), where an array of goods ranging from shoes to copper kettles to golden ornaments was produced for the use of members of the janissary corps.[97] In the Arsenal, *acemi oğlan* were employed as carpenters in shipbuilding; the great architect Mimar Sinan (1490–1588) originally had served an apprenticeship in this craft.[98] Other *acemi oğlan* learned the craft of cannon foundry in the Tophane, the central barracks and arsenal of the Ottoman artillery. Apart from these manufacturing activities, *acemi oğlan* were employed in the transport of supplies from Western Anatolia to the capital; they also worked as laborers in the Sultan's gardens and the manifold enterprises associated with the latter.[99]

But many *acemi oğlan*, perhaps the majority, were never trained in any particular craft and served as common laborers. During the construction of the Süleymaniye complex, candidate janissaries transported stone from the quarries surrounding the Sea of Marmara and on Marmara Island, a task considered so unpleasant that it often was assigned to condemned criminals. Since on every construction site, there is a great demand for unskilled labor, *acemi oğlan* probably dug ditches, carried stones and assisted the trained craftsmen in their work.

Good performance as a workman might lead to rapid enrolment as a janissary, since free positions in the corps were sometimes filled with young men who had served on construction sites or similar enterprises.

Mimar Sinan's example shows that rewards for exceptional skill could be spectacular. But for most *acemi oğlan,* their time of labor service was probably a poorly paid period of unmitigated drudgery.

The 'Civilian' Sector

Mobilizing and controlling labor hardly was the unique privilege of the Ottoman state, even though its activities are much better documented than those of private entrepreneurs. Merchants investing capital in production processes and marketing the finished goods were active everywhere in the economy; for example, in seventeenth-century Bursa, in the cotton industry of the Aegean coastlands of Anatolia, and in the mohair production of the Ankara region.[100] Once the kadi registers of Gaziantep and Diyarbakır have been studied, it is probable that another such network will be uncovered, because the traders who supplied French exporting merchants with the coveted *indiennes* must have had some kind of link with the producers. Thus the assumption that the Ottoman state actively discouraged merchant intervention in manufacture in order to protect the craft guilds is no longer tenable.

In seventeenth-century Bursa, the silk merchants, who constituted one of the most economically powerful groups in the city, owned most of the raw silk imported from Iran. But it is not known whether they also controlled the distribution of locally produced silk. Raw silk belonging to merchants was passed out to a sequence of craftsmen.[101] After the spinners had spun a fine silk thread, the twisters twisted two threads together to increase solidity. Subsequently, the thread was dyed. The manufacture of cloth also involved passing the semi-finished fabrics from one group of specialized artisans to the next. Most of the artisans were fully-fledged craftsmen who either worked in their homes or had workshops of their own; thus they cannot be regarded as employees of the merchants. Their dependence on the putting-out merchant seems comparable to the arrangements found in certain industries of late medieval and early modern Europe.[102]

In addition, putting out-merchants also employed women, who for the most part were not guild members. Women dyers are mentioned in the seventeenth-century kadi registers of Bursa.[103] But even earlier, in the middle of the sixteenth century, peasant women spun mohair for merchants established in Ankara.[104] Thus, putting-out merchants, in their search for cheap labor, mobilized rural and urban women, drawing the latter and their families into the market economy.

Another example of merchant-directed manufacturing was found in the Aegean coastlands of Anatolia. Until ca. 1650, cotton cloth woven in the towns of Buldan, Manisa and Denizli was taken to the nearby provincial capital of Tire for dyeing, an expensive operation that was only feasible if merchants intervened in the production process.[105] Presumably, they bought raw cotton from local peasants or tax collectors, had it woven in nearby towns, and then carried to Tire for dyeing. Even less is known about the itineraries followed by the cotton fabrics woven in the region of Bursa; but they also were brought from the villages into the provincial capital for dyeing, and camels heavily laden with cotton cloth formed a tempting booty for marauders.

In addition, craftsmen also sometimes prospered and set up workshops in which they employed hired labor. This prosperity occurred despite state regulations such as the *ihtisab kanunnameleri*, that should have prevented the enrichment of craftsmen.[106] The rules attempted to regulate the quality, price and profit margins and permitted profit margins of a meagre ten percent, or twenty percent in cases when an exceptional amount of effort was expended. Moreover, unlike merchants engaged in long-distance trade, artisans were closely supervised, both by the kadi and a special official known as the *muhtesib*. Enforcement of these regulations was probably not stringent in all cases, and certain craftsmen turned into entrepreneurs. In seventeenth-century Bursa, wealthy tanners converted sheds and gardens into tanneries, and on the strength of these newly established workshops obtained extra shares of the raw skins and hides entering the city, much to the chagrin of their poorer competitors.[107] The latter complained of undue concentration in the tanning industry. Another example concerns certain Jerusalem butchers of the mid-sixteenth century. Some of the most successful members of this craft branched out into trade, obtained the office of market inspector (*muhtesib*) and achieved a position among the city's dominant families. Given the limited number of cases that have turned up to date, the number of successful craftsmen turned entrepreneurs probably was not very high.[108] The Ottoman case resembled early modern Europe, since in both cultures merchants found it easier to assemble the capital necessary for large-scale production than did master artisans. Nonetheless, we should not forget the occasional transitions from craft production to entrepreneurship.

Apart from organizing the labor of independent artisans, Ottoman manufacturers also employed hired laborers, about whom we know little. In sixteenth- and seventeenth-century Bursa, established master artisans tried to limit the number of competitors by complaining against supposedly unskillful members of the craft setting up their own shops. At the same time, artisans unable to establish themselves in the center of the city migrated to more outlying areas, where subsidiary 'business districts' sprang into existence.[109] In one case, when a master wished to hire laborers, the matter was arranged through the *ehl-i hibre* or experienced guild masters.[110]

Not all migrants came to the cities to find year-round employment. Temporary migration also occurred as inhabitants of villages and small towns came to İstanbul for seasonal work. For example, craftsmen who specialized in the preparation of wax from the fat of slaughtered sheep did most of their work in Rodosçuk-Tekirdağ, one of the subsidiary ports of İstanbul.[111] They delivered wax and animals to the Ottoman court and the janissary barracks in the capital, which means at least some of these people traveled to İstanbul at fairly regular intervals. But their families lived at a distance, in Thessaly, where the craftsmen were recorded for tax-paying purposes. Thus, they must have returned to their homes with some regularity. The artisans' families may have supplemented their income by small-scale agriculture. It is probable, though not certain, that some of these migrant craftsmen were employed as wage laborers by master wax manufacturers in Rodosçuk-Tekirdağ, who controlled the local manufactory or *şemhane*. Thus, the labor supply at the disposal of manufacturers was expanded by drawing rural people into paid employment.

CONCLUSION

When preparing this survey, a serious difficulty was encountered— source materials are so scarce that it is hard to establish a series of 'turning points' that allow us to place the history of Ottoman manufacturing in a chronological framework; or, to put it differently, it is hard to determine the conjunctures of Ottoman manufacturing as a whole. The authors of earlier monographs have acted on the often implicit assumption that the fate of the industry that they happened to be studying, particularly the Bursa silk manufactures, reflected the fate of Ottoman industry as a whole. This is probably not realistic, but alternative suggestions remain no less hypothetical.

For the period before 1550–70, information is more or less limited to the Bursa area, apart from a late fifteenth-century document on the trade of the Black Sea.[112] This customs register indicates the existence of Anatolian craft production directed toward internal and external trade, but it tells us absolutely nothing about capital investment or the deployment of labor. The Ottoman administration became considerably more bureaucratized during the middle years of the sixteenth century, and this explains the abrupt increase of record keeping. But the last quarter of the sixteenth century, as is well known, was also a period of exceptional difficulties. In the later years of Kanuni Süleyman, struggles for the throne among his sons formed the starting point for serious political crisis, while only a few years later, English ships entered the Mediterranean in large numbers, importing cheap woolen fabrics and increasing the problems of Salonica cloth manufacturers. After 1590, the Celali rebellions created a general climate of insecurity, with negative repercussions upon manufacturing in poorly defended small towns and villages. But in the absence of data on pre-1550s craft production, we cannot really tell which crafts were strongly affected and which ones suffered less. It is quite possible that certain phenomena, which we regard as crisis symptoms, had existed in earlier times as well, and should be considered part of the economy *ancien style*.

Nor do we know very much about the duration of this turn-of-the-century crisis. There is some evidence for economic revival after 1650, but its timing and locale have been studied only to a limited extent.[113] Large cities such as Ankara and Kayseri apparently recovered quite well, particularly since their respective regions were too remote from the coast for demand from İstanbul to exert too much pressure. İzmir grew into a major regional center, as the cotton of its hinterland attracted an increasing number of European merchants.[114] The war of 1683–1699 probably cut short this revival, but since the matter has never been studied, the damage can only be hypothesized.

After 1700, we enter into the long boom of the early eighteenth century that, particularly after 1730, coincides with a period of economic revival in Europe.[115] This evidence argues against a very close connection of the Ottoman and European economies since, André Gunder Frank argues, dependent economies prosper when the capitalist center is going through a major crisis and links to colonies and semi-colonies are weakened in consequence.[116] But it is still too early to say which of the post-1700 growth spurts we observe are genuine, and which ones are merely instances of lop-sided growth, as sectors newly integrated within a European-based trade network expanded at the expense of the more balanced economy of earlier periods.

Even worse, we cannot tell whether there was a significant change in labor recruitment during the sixteenth and seventeenth centuries. The Bursa anomaly of a slave-based industry almost certainly disappeared in the seventeenth century, as the city lost its position in international trade and became an ordinary albeit large provincial town. As a working hypothesis, we can assume that merchant control of cotton weaving expanded wherever this cloth entered international trade. İzmir and its hinterland presumably were affected in the later seventeenth century while the expansion of *indiennes* production in eighteenth-century Northern Syria and Southern Anatolia should have led to the rising importance of putting-out merchants. But this is not certain since Ottoman craft guilds were quite flexible, and production could be increased without necessarily destroying the guild framework.[117]

Where other regions of the Ottoman Empire are concerned, there is little evidence of changes in civilian labor recruitment during the period under study. But we have seen that the Ottoman state, which acted as the single most important coordinator of craft labor, expanded recruiting in wartime and loosened its grip over the civilian economy in times of peace. Perhaps periods of extraordinary construction activities such as the 1550s or early 1600s were, from an economic viewpoint, equivalent to a (minor) war. When the state channeled all available resources toward war (and construction), an economic downturn was the result. Studies of early modern Europe have pointed to famines and wars as factors influencing economic conjuncture.[118] For the Ottoman context, we do not possess any evidence that fairly frequent plague epidemics occasioned major economic downturns, but things are quite different where wars are concerned. It is quite possible that population expansion, the importation of Spanish silver and European preindustrial competition were not alone in bringing about the major economic crisis of the late sixteenth and early seventeenth centuries. As important, if not more so, was the effect of war-time mobilization, the long and intensive wars on the Habsburg and Iranian frontiers that necessitated widespread mobilization of labor, and the low to non-existent payment for services that prevented the emergence of a wartime boom.[119]

If this hypothesis is at all sensible, I am strengthening the case of those who assume that sixteenth- and seventeenth-century contacts with the emerging capitalism of Europe were as yet too limited and marginal to substantially affect more than a few 'special case' industries working primarily for an affluent clientele. The provincial networks of Ottoman merchants were as yet scarcely affected, which would explain later industrial revivals.[120] On the other hand, by stressing the role of war in determining economic conjuncture, I place the Ottoman Empire on the same plane as France or the Habsburg Empire. After all, the latter two states during the seventeenth century also overburdened their tax-paying peasantries to pay for war, state building and, last but not least, extensive public construction.[121] All three states were large, given the technical possibilities of the age, the Ottoman Empire more so than the others.[122] This situation made Ottoman warfare more expensive than it would otherwise have been. For while the Ottoman army campaigning in Hungary was provisioned from Rumelia and other provinces close to the front, many soldiers, and an appreciable share of the artisans drafted to serve them, came from İstanbul or even Anatolia.[123] But more importantly, in spite of many political and ideological differences, the three states in question were embarked upon comparable projects. All three governments were in the process of creating a balance between political forces representing the center and the provinces respectively, and fostering prestigious high cultures that were to help secure state survival in times of political crisis.[124] Given these circumstances, it would not be astonishing if France, the Habsburg state, and the Ottoman Empire all paid the price for war and state building in the form of economic crises.

NOTES

1. İnalcık (1979); Fekete (1949).

2. Ergenç (1975).

3. Valensi (1969).

4. Fukasawa (1987); Bayly (1989).

5. Faroqhi (1983), 215 ff..

6. Finkel (1988), vol. 1, 119–208.

7. Braudel (1979), vol. 2, 12.

8. İslamoğlu-İnan (1987), 116 ff.

9. On the difficulty involved in obtaining cash for the payment of soldiers, see Sahillioğlu (1970).

10. Barkan (1972,1979), vol. 1, 347.

11. Cafer Çelebi, Crane (ed.), (1987), 66; Barkan (1972,1979), vol. 1, 107.

12. Barkan (1972, 1979), vol. 1, 95, 99–101.

13. Barkan (1949–50, 1951–52, 1953-54), vol. 11, 545.

14. 'Campaigns and victories' (*sefer ve zafer*) among Turkish intellectuals has about the same meaning as our 'king and battle history'.

15. Jacquart (1975), 241 ff.

16. Raymond (1973–74), vol. 1, 85–86 discusses short-lived crises in 1678, 1687, 1689–90, the first of which preceded the outbreak of war by five years.

17. For a critical evaluation of the notion that the Ottoman Empire constituted a perfect war machine compare also an unpublished paper by Caroline Finkel, held at the symposium 'Legalismus und Herrschafts-legitimation im Osmanischen Reich und in der frühen Türkischen Republik, ca. 1500 bis 1940' (Bochum, Federal Republic of Germany (FRG), 1988).

18. Genç (1984).

19. For the consequences of this neglect as far as the hajj route was concerned, compare Barbir (1980), 137.

20. Braudel (1979), vol. 2, 259 ff. The model was originally invented by Hubert Bourgin.

21. This characteristic feature has been much emphasized by Mehmet Genç, particularly in the paper he gave at the Fourth Congress on the Social and Economic History of Turkey (Munich, 1986).

22. Sahillioğlu (1985).

23. Sahillioğlu (1985), 57.

24. Sahillioğlu (1985), 92.

25. İnalcık (1980–81), 84; Sahillioğlu (1985), 92–95.

26. İnalcık (1980–81), 89.

27. Sahillioğlu (1985), 86, 89.

28. Ergenç (1973); Jennings (1972); Göyünç (1969); Abdel Nour (1982); Masters (1988). Marcus (1989).

29. Sahillioğlu (1985), 47.

30. Gerber (1988).

31. Gerber (1988), 21.

32. Bennassar & Bennassar (1989).

33. Bennassar & Bennassar (1989), 393, 388.

34. Bennassar & Bennassar (1989), 376.

35. Bennassar & Bennassar (1989), 376.

36. Bachrouch (1977), 66. Nor was slave labor of major significance in the Arsenal of Tunis since most Tunisian ships were not constructed locally, but acquired by purchase or as booty.

37. Cafer Çelebi, Crane (ed.), 13.

38. İnalcık (1973), 78.

39. Toledano (1982), 8.

40. İnalcık (1973), 112–113.

41. İnalcık (1969–70).

42. Tansel (1969), 69.

43. Faroqhi (1980), 71.

44. Barkan (1972, 1979), vol. 1, 97.

45. Barkan (1972, 1979), vol. 1, 98.

46. Barkan (1972, 1979), vol. 2, 292.

47. Barkan (1972, 1979), vol. 2, 292. The author of the document does not refer to this issue, but speaks of bad harvests and increased demand for building labor as reasons for the wage increase; the latter supposedly was due to the construction of high-rise buildings in the Jewish quarters.

48. Barkan (1972, 1979), vol. 1, 1–45 contains a discussion of the account books that have survived from the Süleymaniye construction.

49. Cafer Çelebi, Crane (ed.), 69.

50. Barkan (1972, 1979), vol. 2, 291.

51. Barkan (1972, 1979), vol. 2, 284.

52. *Tarama Sözlüğü* (1963–77), vol. 3, 1793.

53. Çizakça (1981), 775.

54. Bostan (1985), 113.

55. Çizakça (1981), 784.

56. Barkan (1972, 1979), vol. 2, 292; Bostan (1985), 117.

57. Kütükoğlu (1978), 22; Kütükoğlu (1983), 53. I assume that the *dirhem* mentioned here is equivalent to 4.81g as calculated by Hinz (1955), 5.

58. Braudel (1979), vol. 1, 106.

59. Kütükoğlu (1983), 324.

60. Uzunçarşılı (1943, 1944), vol. 1, 368.; Mantran (1962) 389 ff.; Gerber (1988), 45–48.

61. Çorum kadı sicili of 1595/96, Çorum Belediye Kütüphanesi.

62. Uzunçarşılı (1943, 1944), vol. 1, 369.

63. Bostan (1985), 328 ff.

64. Bostan (1985), 329.

65. Compare Faroqhi (1980), 71 for the drafting of artisans from Egypt.

66. Rogers (1986), 144–145.

67. Uzunçarşılı (1943, 1944), vol. 1, 273 ff.; Braude (1979).

68. Uzunçarşılı (1943, 1944), vol. 1, 276.

69. Uzunçarşılı (1943, 1944), vol. 1, 276.

70. Sella (1968); Braude (1979).

71. Sella (1968); Rapp (1976).

72. Braude (1979), 446–447.

73. Faroqhi (1980), 68.

74. Faroqhi (1980), 69.

75. Uzunçarşılı (1943, 1944), vol. 1, 276.

76. Uzunçarşılı (1943, 1944), vol. 1, 276.

77. Uzunçarşılı (1943, 1944), vol. 1, 282–284.

78. Faroqhi (1984) 129–130.

79. Güçer (1964), 28–36.

80. On baking, the most comprehensive account relates to mid-sixteenth century Jerusalem: Cohen (1989), 98–118.

81. Barkan (1972, 1979), vol. 1, 362–365; on similar arrangements in textile production, see Dalsar (1960), 228.

82. Güçer (1962–63) on salt; Faroqhi (1979) on alum; as yet there is no comprehensive monograph on saltpeter.

83. Faroqhi (1984), 174, 180.

84. Beldiceanu (1964), vol. 2, 89 ff. demonstrates the complexity of the situation. Concerning the rights of the Sultan see p. 93.

85. Sahillioğlu (1962–63), 153.

86. Faroqhi (1979), 167.

87. Barkan (1943), 72.

88. For one example among many, compare Goubert (1968), 150 ff.

89. Faroqhi (1984), 186–187.

90. On the general rule that low prices indicate a sluggish commercial life, compare Braudel (1979), vol. 2, 43.

91. Faroqhi (1984), 185.

92. Gerber (1988), 45 ff.

93. Gökbilgin (1957), 30 ff.

94. Bostan (1985), 329.

95. Gerber (1988), 26.

96. Barkan (1972, 1979), vol. 1, 108.

97. Uzunçarşılı (1943, 1944), vol. 1, 40–42, 57–60; Barkan (1972, 1979), vol. 1, 110–111.

98. Bostan (1985), 106.

99. Barkan (1972, 1979), vol. 1, 110.

100. Faroqhi (1989).

101. Fukasawa (1987); Gerber (1988), 65.

102. For one example among many, compare Goubert (1968), 159–160.

103. Gerber (1988), 65.

104. Faroqhi (1989), 115.

105. Faroqhi (1989), 116.

106. İnalcık (1973), 154.

107. Başbakanlık Arşivi, Şikayet Defteri No. 3, p 100 (1065/1654–55).

108. Cohen (1989), 31 ff.

109. İnalcık (1969), 117.

110. Gerber (1988), 66.

111. İstanbul Başbakanlık Arşivi, Mühimme Defteri 85, p 97 (1040/1630–31).

112. İnalcık (1979).

113. Compare Faroqhi (1987), 202–221.

114. Goffman (1990).

115. Genç (1984); Labrousse (1970a).

116. Frank (1967), 33.

117. Todorov (1967–68), 20 ff.

118. Labrousse (1970b), vol. 2, 529–566. An empirical study of the kadi registers of seventeenth-century Manisa, an important cotton-producing center, should permit the testing of my hypothesis as far as the Aegean region is concerned. A study of the Gaziantep and Diyarbakır registers unfortunately awaits the advent of more peaceful conditions in the region.

119. Genç (1984).

120. Braudel (1979), vol. 3, 414–415.

121. Steensgaard (1978).

122. French historians have frequently insisted upon the difficulties resulting from the (by pre-industrial European standards) extended size of the French kingdom. Compare Braudel (1979), vol. 3, 269 ff. Evans (1989) deals with the integration of the Habsburg territories.

123. Finkel (1988), 308 emphasizes that provinces close to the Hungarian front were the source of most Ottoman supplies during the 'Long War'.

124. Compare Fleischer (1986) on the high culture of the sixteenth-century Ottoman Empire and Evans (1989), 227–312 on the cultural integration of Habsburg territories during the seventeenth century.

REFERENCES

Abdel Nour, Antoine
    1982   *Introduction à l'histoire urbaine de la Syrie ottomane (XVIᵉ–XVIIIᵉ siècle)*. Beirut.

Bachrouch, Taoufik
    1977   *Formation sociale barbaresque et pouvoir à Tunis au XVIIᵉ siècle*. Faculté des Lettres et Sciences Humaines de Tunis, IV, vol. XXIII, Tunis.

Barbir, Karl K.
    1980   *Ottoman Rule in Damascus, 1708–1758*. Princeton.

Barkan, Ömer Lütfi
    1943   *XV. ve XVI. ıncı Asırlarda Osmanlı İmparatorluğunda Ziraî Ekonominin Hukukî ve Malî Esasları*. İstanbul.

Barkan, Ömer Lütfi
    1949–50,
    1951–52,
    1953–54   "Osmanlı İmparatorluğunda bir İskân ve Kolonizasyon Metodu Olarak Sürgünler", *İstanbul Üniversitesi İktisat Fakültesi Mecmuası*, XI, XIII, and XV.

Barkan, Ömer Lütfi
    1972,
    1979   *Süleymaniye Cami ve İmareti İnşaatı (1550–1557)*. 2 vols., Ankara.

Başbakanlık Arşivi (İstanbul),
            Şikayet Defteri.
            Mühimme Defteri.

Bayly, C.A.
    1989   *Imperial Meridian. The British Empire and the World.*
            London, New York.

Beldiceanu, Nicoara
    1964   *Les actes des premiers sultans conservés dans les
            manuscrits de la Bibliothèque Nationale à Paris.* 2 Vols.,
            Paris, The Hague.

Bennassar, Bartolomé & Bennassar, Lucile
    1989   *Les Chrétiens d'Allah, L'histoire extraordinaire des
            renégats, XVIᵉ–XVIIᵉ siècles.* Paris.

Bostan, İdris
    1985   "XVII. Asırda Tersâne-i amire," unpublished Ph.D.
            dissertation, İstanbul University.

Braude, Benjamin
    1979   "International Competition and Domestic Cloth in the
            Ottoman Empire 1500–1650: A Study in Undevelopment,"
            Review, II.

Braudel, Fernand
    1979   *Civilisation matérielle, Économie et Capitalisme, XVᵉ–
            XVIIIᴇ siècle.* 3 vols.: *Les structures du quotidien, Le
            possible et l'impossible; Les jeux de l'échange; Le temps du
            monde.* Paris.

[Cafer, Çelebi]
    1987   *Risale-i Mi'mariyye, An Early Seventeenth-Century
            Ottoman Treatise on Architecture.* Ed., tr. by Howard
            Crane, Leiden, New York.

Cohen, Amnon
    1989   *Economic Life in Ottoman Jerusalem.* Cambridge.

Çizakça, Murat
    1981   "Ottomans and the Mediterranean: An Analysis of the Ottoman Shipbuilding Industry as Reflected by the Arsenal Registers of İstanbul 1529–1650", in Rosalba Ragosta, Luigi de Rosa eds., *Le genti del mare mediterraneo*, 2 vols., Naples, vol. 2.

Dalsar, Fahri
    1960   *Türk Sanayi ve Ticaret Tarihinde Bursa'da İpekçilik.* İstanbul.

Ergenç, Özer
    1973   "1580–1596 Yılları Arasında Ankara ve Konya Şehirlerinin Mukayeseli İncelenmesi Yoluyla Osmanlı Şehirlerinin Kurumları ve Sosyo-ekonomik Yapısı Üzerine bir Deneme", unpublished Ph.D. thesis, Ankara University.

Ergenç, Özer
    1975   "1600–1615 Yılları Arasında Ankara İktisadi Tarihine Ait Araştırmalar" in Osman Okyar, Ünal Nalbantoğlu, eds., *Türkiye İktisat Tarihi Semineri, Metinler Araştırmalar.* Ankara.

Evans, Robert J.W.
    1989   *Das Werden der Habsburgermonarchie 1550–1700, Gesellschaft, Kultur, Institutionen.* Vienna, Cologne.

Faroqhi, Suraiya
    1979   "Alum Production and Alum Trade in the Ottoman Empire (about 1560–1830)", *Wiener Zeitschrift für die Kunde des Morgenlandes.*

Faroqhi, Suraiya
    1980   "Textile Production in Rumeli and the Arab Provinces: Geographical Distribution and Internal Trade (1560-1650)", *Osmanlı Araştırmaları*, I.

Faroqhi, Suraiya
    1983   "Die osmanische Handelspolitik des frühen 17. Jahrhunderts zwischen Dubrovnik und Venedig", in Grete

Klingenstein et al. eds., *Wiener Beiträge zur Geschichte der Neuzeit, 10, Das Osmanische Reich und Europa 1683 bis 1789: Konflikt, Entspannung und Austausch,* Wien.

Faroqhi, Suraiya
1984   *Towns and Townsmen of Ottoman Anatolia. Trade, Crafts and Food Production in an Urban Setting, 1520–1650.* Cambridge.

Faroqhi, Suraiya
1987   *Men of Modest Substance. House Owners and House Property in Seventeenth-Century Ankara and Kayseri.* Cambridge.

Faroqhi, Suraiya
1989   "Merchant Networks and Ottoman Craft Production (Sixteenth to Seventeenth Centuries)", in Yuzo Itagaki, Masao Mori, Takeshi Yukawa eds., *Urbanism in Islam, The Proceedings of the International Conference on Urbanism in Islam (ICUIT),* Oct. 22–28, 1989. 5 vols., Tokyo: Research Project "Urbanism in Islam" and the Middle Eastern Culture Center in Japan, vol. 1.

Fekete, Lajos
1949   "Osmanlı Türkleri ve Macarlar, 1366–1699," *Belleten,* XIII.

Finkel, Caroline
1988   *The Administration of Warfare: The Ottoman Military Campaigns in Hungary, 1593–1606.* 2 vols., Vienna.

Fleischer, Cornell
1986   *Bureaucrat and Intellectual in the Ottoman Empire. The Historian Mustafa Ali (1541–1600).* Princeton.

Frank, André Gunder
1967   *Capitalism and Underdevelopment in Latin America. Historical Studies of Chile and Brazil.* New York, London.

Fukasawa, Katsumi
1987   *Toilerie et commerce du Levant d'Alep à Marseille.* Paris.

Genç Mehmet
1984   "XVIII. Yüzyılda Osmanlı Ekonomisi ve Savaş", *Yapıt*, vol.
          49, no. 4, 50, no. 5.

Gerber, Haim
1988   *Economy and Society in an Ottoman City: Bursa,
          1600–1700.* Jerusalem.

Goffman, Daniel
1990   *Izmir and the Levantine World 1550–1650.* Seattle and
          London.

Goubert, Pierre
1968   *100 000 provinciaux aux XVIIe siècle, Beauvais et le
          Beauvaisis de 1600 à 1730.* Paris.

Gökbilgin, Tayyip
1957   *Rumeli'de Yürükler, Tatarlar ve Evlâd-i Fatihân.*
          İstanbul.

Göyünç, Nejat
1969   *XVI. Yüzyılda Mardin Sancağı.* İstanbul.

Güçer, Lütfi
1962–63 "XV–XVII Asırlarda Osmanlı İmparatorluğunda Tuz İnhisarı
          ve Tuzlaların İşletme Nizami", *İstanbul Üniversitesi İktisat
          Fakültesi Mecmuası*, vol. 23, no. 1–4.

Güçer, Lütfi
1964   *XVI–XVII. Asırlarda Osmanlı İmparatorluğunda
          Hububat Meselesi ve Hububattan Alınan Vergiler.*
          İstanbul.

Hinz, Walter
1955   "Islamische Masse und Gewichte umgerechnet ins
          metrische System" in Bertold Spuler ed., *Handbuch der
          Orientalistik,* suppl. 1,1. Leiden.

İnalcık, Halil
1969   "Capital Formation in the Ottoman Empire", *The Journal of
          Economic History*, XIX.

İnalcık, Halil
1969–70　"The Policy of Mehmet II Toward the Greek Population of İstanbul and the Byzantine Buildings of the City", *Dumbarton Oaks Papers.*

İnalcık, Halil
1973　*The Ottoman Empire, The Classical Age 1300–1600.* London.

İnalcık, Halil
1979　"The Question of the Closing of the Black Sea Under the Ottomans", *Symposium on the Black Sea, Birmingham, March 18–20, 1978, Archeion Pontou.*

İnalcık, Halil
1980–81　"Osmanlı Idare, Sosyal ve Ekonomik Tarihiyle Ilgili Belgeler: Bursa Kadı Sicillerinden Seçmeler", *Belgeler,* X.

İslamoğlu-İnan, Huri
1987　"State and Peasants in the Ottoman Empire: A Study of Peasant Economy in North-Central Anatolia During the Sixteenth Century", in Huri İslamoğlu-İnan, ed. *The Ottoman Empire and The World Economy.* Cambridge.

Jacquart, Jean
1975　"Immobilisme et catastrophes 1560–1660" in Georges Duby, Armand Wallon, Emmanuel Le Roy Ladurie, eds. *Histoire de la France rurale.* 4 vols., Paris, vol. 2.

Jennings, Ronald
1972　"The Judicial Registers (Şeri Mahkeme Sicilleri) of Kayseri (1590–1630) as a Source for Ottoman History", unpublished Ph.D. dissertation, University of California, Los Angeles.

Kütükoğlu, Mübahat S.
1978　"1009 (1600) Tarihli Narh Defterine göre İstanbul'da Çeşidli Eşya ve Hizmet Fiatları", *Tarih Enstitüsü Dergisi.*

Kütükoğlu, Mübahat S.
1983　*Osmanlılarda Narh Müessesesi ve 1640 Tarihli Narh Defteri.* İstanbul.

Labrousse, Ernest
    1970a   "L'expansion agricole: La montée de la production", in Fernand Braudel and Ernest Labrousse eds., *Histoire économique et sociale de la France.* 4 vols., vol. 2, Paris.

Labrousse, Ernest
    1970b   "Les ruptures périodiques de la prospérité: les crises économiques du XVIIIe siècle", in Fernand Braudel and Ernest Labrousse eds., *Histoire économique et sociale de la France.* 4 vols., vol. 2, Paris.

Mantran, Robert
    1962   *İstanbul dans la seconde moitié du XVIIe siècle, Essai d'histoire institutionelle, économique et sociale.* Paris.

Marcus, Abraham
    1989   *The Middle East on the Eve of Modernity. Aleppo in the Eighteenth Century.* New York.

Masters, Bruce
    1988   *The Origins of Western Economic Dominance in the Middle East, Mercantilism and the Islamic Economy in Aleppo, 1600–1750.* New York, London.

Rapp, Richard Tilden
    1976   *Industry and Economic Decline in Seventeenth-Century Venice.* Cambridge, MA.

Raymond, André
    1973–74   *Artisans et commerçants au Caire au XVIIIe siècle.* 2 vols., Damascus.

Rogers, Michael
    1986   "Ottoman Luxury Traders and their Regulation", in Hans Georg Majer ed., *Osmanistische Studien zur Wirtschafts- und Sozialgeschichte, in memoriam Vanco Boskov.* Wiesbaden.

Sahillioğlu, Halil
    1962–63   "Bir Mültezim Zimem Defterine göre XV. Yüzyıl Sonunda Osmanlı Darphane Mukataaları", *İstanbul Universitesi İktisat Fakültesi Mecmuası*, vol. 23, no. 1–4.

Sahillioğlu, Halil
    1970   "Sıvış Year Crises in the Ottoman Empire", in M.A. Cook
              ed., Studies in the Economic History of the Middle East,
              from the Rise of Islam to the Present Day. Oxford.

Sahillioğlu, Halil
    1985   "Slaves in the Social and Economic Life of Bursa in the Late
              Fifteenth and Early Sixteenth Centuries", Turcica, XVII.

Sella, Domenico
    1968   "The Rise and Fall of the Venetian Woolen Industry", in
              Brian Pullan ed., Crisis and Change in the Venetian
              Economy in the Sixteenth and Seventeenth Centuries.
              London.

Steensgard, Niels
    1978   "The Seventeenth-Century Crisis", in Geoffrey Parker,
              Lesley M. Smith eds., The General Crisis of the Seventeenth
              Century. London.

Tansel, Selâhattin
    1969   Yavuz Sultan Selim. Ankara.

Tarama Sözlüğü
    1963–77   XIII. Yüzyıldan Beri Türkiye Türkçesiyle Yazılmış
              Kitaplardan Toplanan Tanıklarıyla Tarama Sözlüğü. 8
              Vols., Ankara.

Todorov, Nicolay
    1967–68   "19.cu Yüzyılın İlk Yarısında Bulgaristan Esnaf Teşkilatında
              Bazı Karakter Değişmeleri", İstanbul Üniversitesi İktisat
              Fakültesi Mecmuası, vol. 27, no. 1–2.

Toledano, Ehud R.
    1982   The Ottoman Slave Trade and Its Suppression 1840–1890.
              Princeton.

Uzunçarşılı, İsmail Hakkı
    1943–44   Osmanlı Devleti Teşkilatından Kapukulu Ocakları. 2 vols.,
              Ankara.

Valensi, Lucette
    1969   "Islam et capitalisme: production et commerce des
                chéchias en Tunisie et en France aux XVIIIe–XIXe siècles",
                Revue d'histoire moderne et contemporaire, XVII.

Veinstein, Gilles
    1988   "Du marché urbain au marché du camp: l'institution
                ottomane des orducu". In Abdeljelil Temimi, ed. *Mélanges
                Professeur Robert Mantran,* Zaghouan.

3

Ottoman Industry in the Eighteenth Century: General Framework, Characteristics, and Main Trends

Mehmet Genç

Changes that occurred in Ottoman industry in the eighteenth century do not bear any resemblance to the explosive industrial growth then occurring in Western Europe. Ottoman industry was neither totally stagnant nor did it evolve in a linear, uniform fashion over the course of the century. On the contrary, Ottoman industry displayed a complex development pattern under the impact of various regional influences and in different sectors of the industry; sometimes it expanded or shrunk, and was then revitalized, and at other times it remained totally stagnant. Nonetheless, patterns of development do not show trends, which potentially might have led to modern economic growth.

Obviously, the Ottoman economic system itself was not completely immune to the changes occurring externally. Still, principles that the Ottoman state itself relied on and imposed on the overall economy, and on industry in particular, remained immutable. This immutability can be observed best at times when pressure was exerted to motivate change.

One of the principles that the classical Ottoman system relied on is
known as *provisionism*, that is, the maintenance of a steady supply so that
all goods and services were cheap, plentiful, and of good quality. With
respect to foreign trade, provisionism sought to keep the supply of goods
and services to the internal market at an optimal level. Export was not
encouraged, but rather curtailed by prohibitions, quotas, and taxes.
Imports, by contrast, were fostered and facilitated.

Ottoman state provisionism did not require an import substitution
policy as long as imports helped maintain the steady supply of goods and
services. At times when imports could not fulfill this function, import
substitution policies were put in operation. Industries that provided arms
and equipment to the Ottoman military is a typical example of this
practice. In this sector, sustaining all the necessary installations to avoid
any dependence on foreign armaments was crucial.

The second principle that ruled Ottoman economic policy was
traditionalism. We may summarize this as the tendency to preserve the
existing conditions, and look to the past for models instead of searching
for a new equilibrium when changes occurred. Traditionalism found its
expression in the time-honored motto that one should not work against
what comes from the olden time: *kadimden olagelene aykırı iş
yapılmaması*. It remained a vital component of the referential framework
of the Ottoman economic system that remained unchanged during the
eighteenth century.

Fiscalism was the third principle guiding Ottoman economic policy
decisions and can be summarized as the maximization of treasury income
and the effort to prevent it from falling below already-attained levels.
Parallel to the rhythm of increase in the production capacity of the
Ottoman economy as well as in the degree of monetization, increases in
the income of the treasury were extremely difficult and slow to achieve.
For that reason, Ottoman fiscalism developed in the direction of
preventing a fall in incomes and reducing expenses. A fisco-centrism
evolved and was so rigid that it viewed all economic activity only in terms
of the tax income they would yield.

The *mirî mübayaa* regime was one measure to reduce expenses.
This policy imposed a tax-like levy to facilitate the provision of goods and
services for the state at a price usually lower than the market prices (and
sometimes even below production costs). Since the policy did not
concern imports, an import substitution policy was implemented when the
volume of imports threatened the state's fiscal standing. At such times, the
state did not consider pursuing a strong protectionist customs policy
because this would lead to increases in prices on the internal market.

Among the institutions established according to fiscalism during the eighteenth century, we need to mention the life-term tax farming system (*malikâne sistemi*), which had an impact on the entire economy, including industry.[1] In this system, the collection of public revenues was distributed as life-term tax farms (*malikâne*). The contractor of the public revenues (*mültezim*) paid the Treasury a fixed annual tax that annually was confirmed by the state. This system sought to encourage the contractors to increase the production of the resources from which they derived tax revenues. This arrangement ensured the growth of tax revenues derived from such resources and that the amount above the fixed amount would be left to the contractors. The *mültezim* would pay in advance for the source of the revenues derived from such taxes; this cash advance, known as *muaccele*, was the actual capitalization of his prospective profits. The amount of the cash advance was settled at auction to the highest bidder; a steady and progressively growing source of income to the Treasury. The contractors increased production, causing the tax revenues to increase and, accordingly, the actual capital. This policy, which created an active market for contractors, was put into operation in 1695 and was expanded in the eighteenth century to the extent that it affected all taxable economic activities.

This system had some positive economic impact, even though somewhat less than anticipated by the government. New contractors helped to improve productivity in the *malikâne*s they bought; they maintained security, provided credits, and even made long-term investments. Their attitude was very different from that of earlier tax collectors. Take, for example, the activities of a bureaucrat who bought the stamp duties of printed cotton cloth and dyehouse workshops in Tokat in the form of *malikâne*. In addition to maintaining these establishments, where a considerable amount of cotton cloth and printed cotton cloth was manufactured, he established a large dyeworks factory in 1726 where he located all the dyers.[2] New contractors who came from the ranks of the bureaucracy and the military thus had a chance to participate in mercantile activities. Nevertheless, this did not lead to the emergence of capitalist entrepreneurs. They remained as wealthy rentier bureaucrats; that is, the attitudes of the military elite and bureaucracy remained unchanged. *Malikâne*-owners who gradually turned into rentiers started to sub-contract their tax-collecting duties to second or even third parties. Thus the system helped to increase the burden of taxes by transferring the surplus from the productive to the unproductive classes.

Some other negative effects of fiscalism can be observed in the widespread penetration of the lower-ranking members of the military into areas of economic activity. We may call this the "militarization" or the "bureaucratization" of the economy. Here's how it worked: the genuine financial needs of the bureaucracy and the military, as well as the swelling of the permanent government cadres as a result of nepotism, continuously tended to surpass the bounds of the income coming into the Treasury. To provide additional revenues, a custom practiced since the seventeenth century became widespread during the eighteenth century. Known as "*hazine mande*", this policy encouraged low-ranking members of the military to bequeath their salaries to the Treasury. In turn, the Treasury assigned these persons to new positions in various areas of the economy, with titles such as *katip, dellal, bekçi,* and *gözcü*. Others included the artisanal administrative positions, starting in İstanbul, this practice became widespread in large- and even medium-size cities as administrators, carrying titles such as *kethüda, şeyh* and *yiğitbaşı,* were assigned to artisans.

Ottoman artisanal organizations had possessed considerable autonomy—they had elected their own administrators and paid their salaries. However, they could not resist the intervention of the military under the protection of the Treasury. Thus, they accepted the military into administrative positions in their organizations, believing that they would benefit from the privileges of the former. However, since the new administrators had no actual training or experience in administration, artisanal organizations maintained their traditional administrative framework. A double administration, thus doubly expensive, was established. This new channel, established to derive extra income for providing security for artisanal manufacture, became widespread in the eighteenth century. These newly established ranks and administrative positions then became a new source for taxes and started to be sold as *malikâne*. Artisans, by paying extra fees, employed the security they ensured to strengthen their own monopolies.

This pattern reinforced the tendency of artisans who were involved in the production of the same goods and services to come together in monopolies, a practice that became widespread in the eighteenth century. Rather than resisting, the state assisted, and sometimes promoted, this development. Such monopolistic trends not only would prevent fiscal smuggling and reduce tax-collecting expenses but also, in accordance with provisionism, would assign the production of each good or service to the responsibility of a certain group. Thus, the steady supply and the control over the quality and price of the goods would be assured. Further, since the income and saving capacity of the artisans prevented them from investing in the physical plant, the state itself undertook such investments either directly or through pious foundations (*vakıfs*). In this manner, the state could extract some extra rent in addition to the taxes from artisanal production. Such investments formed part of the general trend in which the economy became more active and gradually expanded during the first half of the eighteenth century. Both in the activities that were expanding mainly for fiscal reasons, and in those that were contracting because of provisionist and protectionist thinking, investments were made in facilities used in the final stages of industrial production (such as dyeing, printing, and finishing/polishing installations as well as in oil, candle, and soap manufactories, and tanneries). As a result of such investments, the control of the state and the pious foundations over manufacturing expanded.

This eighteenth-century development, which combined the three principles that defined the Ottoman economic system on different levels, meant an expansion of existing state control over production into the urban industrial sector.

In industry, the concentration (centralization) of the final stages of production in certain centers under state control, instead of expanding the possibilities for development of these centers as proto-factories, caused their decline. These centers did not undergo organizational changes in terms of labor division, technology, or productivity. Artisanal organization dominated production. Collective working intensified the egalitarian and traditionalist qualities and attitudes of the artisanal organizations. They became more resistant to changes that, elsewhere in the world, would trigger a capitalist transformation. Agents employed to collect the taxes from these centers in the name of the state or the pious foundations also became a force resistant to change. These agents who were mostly owners of *malikânes*, although they maintained their right to collect taxes in their lifetime, did not have any property rights over production.[3] Their concern with production was only fiscal, even fisco-centric; they remained indifferent or hostile to confrontations between producers that might jeopardize their tax revenues.

The changes made by the state in the tax-farming system, and the gradual increase in the capital flow, activities obviously aimed at the development of production, sometimes resulted in its quantitative expansion. But these mergers, designed to increase production, sometimes, at the end of our period, produced stagnation and inertia.

Nevertheless, Ottoman industry did not merely stagnate in the eighteenth century. The 'centralization' sought to confine manufacturing to artisanal production under state control, but fiscality was not easily realized. To escape the pressure and limitations, producers moved to small production centers in distant neighborhoods of the city where such controls had not yet been established. In addition, producers moved in accelerating numbers, during the eighteenth century, towards remote towns and villages in the country.

Rural industry obviously was active before this, but because of the classical Ottoman economic system and the provisionist policy, never had the chance to develop. Factors such as state policies promoting family plots, low labor to land ratios, the nature of agricultural land as state property exempt from confiscation, and state policies restricting the mobility of agricultural workers, all contributed to the underdevelopment of rural industry. Thus, rural industry developed only in mountain villages where agriculture was not possible and animal husbandry dominated, and in some populated areas.

In such rural industry, peasants produced and sold finished goods at local markets. The further expansion of production required the possibility for export, possible only with an active export policy against the mercantilistic and protectionist West. Due to prevailing provisionist policies, however, export was a marginal sector that the state taxed and, most of the time, actively hindered.

The vital condition for the development of rural industry was the readiness of an entrepreneurial group with capital to invest. Such a group, however, did not arise within the Ottoman economic system. To the extent possible, the state tried to control the revenues collected from production targeted for the domestic market, from exchange, and from artisanal production in the cities. Although it did not always attain its goals, the state was not altogether unsuccessful in controlling these revenues. The legitimate profit was calculated to be between five percent to fifteen percent in industrial and commercial transactions, and usually remained below ten percent. Interest, although prohibited by religious law, was common; at least fifteen percent was charged and usually reached twenty to twenty-five percent. With such high interest rates, commercial and industrial credits and capital flow were very limited.

This negative picture was beginning to change in the eighteenth century. Two factors, both of which came from outside, had converging and diverging effects. The first, the military challenge of the West, increased the share of public expenditures in the overall economy.

Ottoman *reaya* became more pressed for extra income in the eighteenth century in order to pay their gradually increasing taxes. The second factor was the increase in the Western interest in commerce. The Ottoman economic system maintained its control and limitations on exports by increasing the export dues from three percent (as fixed by the capitulations) to some fifty percent on goods that were in high demand in the West. But this strategy soon had an impact on the production of these goods, considerably increasing the output of industrial raw materials such as cotton, yarn, dye stuffs, and olive oil. It is not possible to give the exact figures for this increase. However, it can be estimated—cotton production, for example, increased three to four times.

Production of industrial raw materials partly satisfied the peasants' need for extra income. In addition there was some lesser expansion in other areas of rural industry. One example came from the Salonica-Macedonia region. There, production of cotton increased from 2.2 million to 7 million *okka* between 1740 and 1790. Most of this cotton produced was exported unprocessed, but 2 million *okka* of the total was spun into cotton yarn and then half of this cotton was woven in the region. The rest was exported to Central Europe.[4]

Clearly, there is a connection between these figures and the remarkable increase in the number of small towns and villages in the Salonica-Macedonia region that contained finishing plants for operations like the washing of thread, dyeing, and printing. This tendency, especially marked from the second quarter of the eighteenth century onward, which can be regarded as an indication of the development of rural industry towards proto-industry, followed a more or less parallel path with opportunities in foreign markets. Indeed, in the Tokat area, as in the Salonica-Macedonia region, the tendency to take flight to small centers intensified between 1730–1766, when local cotton cloths and calicoes enjoyed a market extending from the vicinity of the Black Sea to Russia and Poland. But from the 1770s, the Northern Black Sea area was left to Russia and this market, though not closed altogether, generally began to shrink. Likewise, the pattern that emerged in the Salonica-Macedonia region after the 1740s lasted until the turn of the nineteenth century. In this region as well, the exportation of thread and coarse cloth came to a halt and the foreign market was closed altogether.

The state intervened in a decisive manner in this effort to reduce output costs by moving outside the tax area which was based in the old centers, all of which had turned into *malikânes*. Entrepreneurs had lowered costs through their evasion of the taxes and restrictive practices of the old centers, and by their use of cheaper labor. Ottoman law previously had punished tax evasion with a tax penalty of 100 percent; the new penalties started at 200 percent and included such incredibly harsh sanctions as confiscation of the produced goods, demolition of the plant, and condemnation of the workers to the galleys.[5] The stern orders clearly and emphatically noted that production intended to meet the local demand of nearby towns and villages should not, in compliance with provisionism, be interfered with by any means. The targets of the prohibitions and punishments were activities that likely were to supply the long distance trade, i.e. those with proto-industrial potential. At first sight, it is difficult to comprehend this stern attitude that, with the pretext that it abandoned traditional locations and customs and reduced tax income, condemned this proto-industrial potential even before it was ever born. However, viewed within the coordinates of the principles I have mentioned, it seems applicable. Here, fiscalism is especially important in shaping a state policy that combines all three principles in varying degrees, forming one of its ever-harsher shifts towards fisco-centrism. And this, to a large extent, is a result of the transformation that the *malikâne* system underwent in the hands of the rentier bureaucrats.

The state not only enacted policies that worked against development of manufacturing, but it also created certain obstacles for capital accumulation that might have prepared the grounds for these developments. The regime of *mirî mübayaa*, mentioned before, tops them all. When the need of the state for goods and services rapidly increased due to military exigencies in the second half of the eighteenth century, and when the state incomes did not increase at the same rate, the *mirî mübayaa* regime was applied more intensively. Those producing or trading in cotton cloth, thread, iron, timber, pitch, hemp etc., were thus further burdened. The equivalent of exacting a progressive tax in kind, the policy had a weakening effect on those sectors most likely to develop.

From the 1770s, more burdens were imposed on those that had some accumulated capital. Not only the *ayans*, but also wealthy merchants were required to equip troops and send them to the front on their own account. And, when the treasury was hard pressed, they provided compulsory loans. Finally, during the period 1770–1810, when finances were in a crisis, the state, perhaps for the first time in its history, began confiscating the inheritance of private individuals who were considered rich.

In these conditions, the obstacles to capital accumulation and investment reached a peak.

As stated, this inimical atmosphere against capitalist development did not affect small-scale, craft production destined for local markets. Craft organizations, as structures compatible with all of the three principles on which the Ottoman economic policy relied, remained the predominant form of organization in Ottoman industry throughout the eighteenth century. Differentiation within craft organizations underwent very few changes during the century. The differentiation between the poorest and the richest artisan in the same activity hardly exceeded 1:4 or 1:7. The largest workshops, those in weaving, food, metal and building material production, rarely exceeded five to twenty workers. State factories too remained small-scale workshops, employing approximately eight to twenty workers within a crafts-type organization and with little division of labor. Even in the arms industry, the cannon and gunpowder factories run with hydraulic or animal power had no establishments exceeding 50 to 100 workers.

Work implements and machines were cheap enough for craftsmen to afford easily. As I have noted, most of the buildings and immobile installations, that were somewhat expensive for the income level of the craftsmen, belonged to the state or the pious foundations (*vakıf*s). Most of those that were private property belonged to members of the military class; and, as the property rights of this class were insecure until the middle of the nineteenth century, they kept oozing into the State or *vakıf* group.

As in the eighteenth century, in compliance with the principles of provisionism, exports were continuously held in check. Ottoman industry enjoyed protection with respect to raw materials, which constituted the biggest item of cost, and to a large extent remained dependent on domestic raw material.

Another feature of Ottoman industry in the eighteenth century is the concentration on the production of ordinary commodities produced for non-luxury consumption: e.g., cotton and woolen cloths, food, metal, building materials, household items, earthen- and wooden-wares. Even in silk, medium quality production, mostly silk and cotton combinations rather than pure and luxury silks, remained dominant.

The organization of production and the quality of the domestic raw material being used provides interesting clues about Ottoman society. It suggests a certain egalitarian structure with respect to artisan and peasant production as well as a more egalitarian income and expenditure structure than we had expected.

On the other hand, there was also an upper-income group that mainly belonged to the military class. Most of the high-quality products consumed by this social layer were imports. The greater part, i.e. three quarters of these imported goods, consisted of fine woolens and quality silks. It was these two products that, for the first time in the early eighteenth century, became subject to attempts at import substitution with state capital.

The importation of quality products was not a new phenomenon. According to the logic of provisionism, since the olden times, obtaining these goods through imports had not been considered harmful in any way. Only the fine woolens used in the manufacture of soldiers' cloths, which required large sums, had been domestically produced. Taking advantage of the presence of qualified personnel specializing in this production— Jews who immigrated from Spain in the fifteenth century—factories were established to produce fine woolens in Salonica. However, this production too was transformed, following the general Ottoman pattern from the seventeenth century onwards, in such a way that it specialized in ordinary commodities for non-luxury production.[6] However, when an attempt at import substitution was put on the agenda in the early eighteenth century, a long period of war (1683–1699) had raised prices and reduced the possibilities of importation. Revenues fell and expenses rose as a consequence of war, but the Palace annually paid 40 to 50,000 *kuruş* for the imported woolens and silks. In short, according to both provisionism and fiscalism, import substitution became a necessity. Two of the three factories treated in this study were established to produce these woolens and silks.[7]

All three factories were established primarily in connection with provisionism and fiscalism, especially with the motive of reducing expenses; this is why providing them with customs protection like their European counterparts was never considered. According to the principles that were relied on, this would have been meaningless and absurd.

As will be seen, those factories could not last long. Could they have survived like those in Colbert's France, Peter the Great's Russia, or Meiji's Japan if they had been protected? Probably not.

STATE INVESTMENTS IN MANUFACTURES

Woolen Cloth Manufacture: 1703

Simple and inexpensive textiles as well as more finished woolens were produced throughout the Ottoman Empire and were especially noted in the Balkans. Even the more simple types of woolen cloth known by the name of *aba* and *kebe* found wide appeal among both the lower and middle social groups who wore them and the middle and even upper classes who used such materials for upholstery. Abundant raw materials and a continually expanding radius of interregional exchange within the Empire, in the Adriatic and with Italy helped boost production of these textiles during the eighteenth century. Marseilles merchants exported large quantities of rough woolens for the clothing of galleon slaves.[8]

The situation of fine textile production, however, was different. Except in the case of woolens manufactured of angora wool, which as a rare fiber had only limited application and market, the Ottoman Empire met its needs for middle- and fine-quality woolens with imports from Western Europe. From the seventeenth century onward, despite state measures to encourage and support industry, Ottoman manufacturing and local products (even those of the Spanish Jewish weavers who had settled in Salonica during the fifteenth and sixteenth century) faced stiff competition from Western Europe's increasingly technologically more advanced woolen industry.[9] In effect, Salonica industry grew less and less competitive because it attempted to survive by continually lowering the quality of its manufactures. For example, although the army alone represented a potential market of between 200,000 to 450,000 *zira* of cloth during the eighteenth century, the actual quality of Ottoman manufactures was so low that soldiers preferred to sell their state-issued stuffs to the poor and buy imports for personal use.[10]

To the degree to which such consumer patterns spread to the middle social classes over the seventeenth century, so foreign imports took an ever greater share of the domestic market. In particular, high-quality woolens from Western Europe constituted fifty percent of the entire quantity of imports. During the war period of 1683–1699, when imports witnessed a severe contraction, the danger of such a dependency on imports, which were widely in demand by the court, the elite, and the military, became apparent. The trade of Venice, then in the enemy camp and the source of twenty-five percent of Ottoman woolen imports, was completely redirected. France, England, and Holland, which accounted for the balance of imports, were at war with each other until well after the 1690s; this also contributed to the overall decline in the amount of woolen imports.[11]

The shortages were so great that for the first time, in 1703, the Grand Vezir Rami Mehmet Pasha issued an order to begin state production of woolens in Edirne and Salonica "so as to make provisions to be self-sufficient of woolens from non-Muslim countries."[12] The first stage of production, realized with the aid of Salonica's Jewish weavers who were considered to have the most technical expertise and experience, lasted but a few months. The insurrection of August 1703 that brought down the Sultan and his Grand Vezir also put an end to this chapter of state sponsored industry.

Yet even this short-lived experiment of several months left a great impression on the French who then were in fierce competition with the English for hegemony in the Ottoman woolen market. Responding in August 18, 1704 to what must have been a previously issued directive by his government, France's representative in the Ottoman Empire communicated:

> With regard to cloth manufactories they feign to have
> established in Edirne and Salonica...the undertaking ran
> aground as the new Sultan took the throne, and so,
> Monseigneur, it is no more...It is very true that they
> manufactured samples of *Londrines*, but of very poor
> quality...Besides, it was not the French who manufactured
> them from what I have gathered so far and if the situation is to
> go on like this, I will comply with the orders of Your Highness
> on the subject.[13]

This state initiative to produce woolens did not, however, rest on a passing fancy of a sultan or vezir. Indeed, stubborn attempts, starting only a few years after, were to be continued over a period of some twenty-five years. On this occasion, however, it was decided that a manufacturing center for the woolen cloth industry was to be constructed in İstanbul so that workmanship, stocks and supplies could be brought under strict control. Thirty-eight of the most successful masters from the Jewish weavers of Salonica were summoned to İstanbul and established in the manufactory.[14] Five French prisoners, known to have skills in weaving, were taken out of their galley chains and put to work at their side. The first products of this enterprise appeared in the fall of 1708. The textiles were crude, of uneven quality and very costly. Realizing that the failure may have been due to the fact that the Salonica masters had become specialized in making low-quality woolen cloth, production was suspended toward the end of the year.

The French ambassador Ferriol, who had been closely following the situation, provided his observations in a letter dated October 17, 1708.

Manufacturing of cloth for the Palace collapsed completely, they sent all the weavers who have worked there back to Salonica, and returned to prison all the Frenchmen who were put back again in galley chains. They were producing cloth which seemed to be extremely coarse as it is cottonned and costs more than 3 piasters a pic.[15]

Nonetheless, contrary to what Ferriol wrote, the endeavor to produce woolens was not abandoned. In early 1709, this project was taken up again, with some important changes and on an even larger scale.

While we are not in possession of more detailed information on earlier state initiatives in industrial organization, the existing data suggest that the type of enterprise pursued until this time was exclusively state managed and made use of essentially Ottoman technology and know-how. From 1709 onward, we come across two important changes. The first relates to the organization of production: rather than being the exclusive prerogative of the state, management was entrusted to an entrepreneur with his own capital and liability along the lines of profit and loss. The second concerns the quality of woolen production: the decision was made to locate and import technological know-how from abroad because it was realized that such skills were not to be found within the empire. The planned manufacturing center sought to produce the woolens most in demand within the Ottoman domestic market (such as *mabut, nim,* and *londrine*).

Beginning in early 1709, a non-Muslim Ottoman, whose name appears in the form of Tişo, or alternately Işon, undertook the role of entrepreneur in the new project. His first task was to bring together the technical staff, machinery, and equipment. Statements of French officials indicate that there was little reason to hope for technological aid from Western European countries at this time, because they were competing for dominance in Ottoman markets. Because of this, and/or because of some other relationships of which we are not aware, Tişo chose Poland as the source for technological know-how. With seven masters and machinery from there, which was installed in the İstanbul manufactory, he went into operation.

In the first stage, Tişo was able to establish a manufacturing unit consisting of seven looms at which 150 workers were employed.[16] In successive years, aiming for optimal scale and volume, the number of looms was increased to sixteen and a dyeworks, and other support facilities were added. Accounts up to the year 1716 show that the project had cost 13,000 *kuruş* from the capital of the entrepreneur himself and 47,600 *kuruş* from state coffers, in addition to the costs of the physical plant and other fixed installations.[17] We can estimate that capital up to the amount of 100,000 *kuruş* was invested in this enterprise. This almost equalled one percent of the state's budget (around 10,000,000 *kuruş* in those years); when a skilled worker's daily wage was less than one third of a *kuruş*, this was not an inconsiderable investment.

In fact, these manufacturing initiatives pursued over a period of thirty years, despite several changes of rulers, must be characterized as a deliberate government policy. Nonetheless, despite the large quantities of cloth woven, this enterprise failed to achieve either the desired quality or price and eventually was abandoned after 1732.

The transformation of the woolen market surely constitutes one of the most important reasons for this failure. British woolens, which had been dominant in the seventeenth century Ottoman market, found a tough competitor in French production of cheap and middle-quality woolens during the eighteenth century. Overall, imports from Western Europe formed nearly fifty percent of the total Ottoman woolens market, with France and Britain in the dominant position.

Table 1A.   Woolen Imports from France

Annual Average in Pieces of Cloth	
1700–1705	10,300
1708–1715	21,800
1716–1720	22,600
1721–1725	24,240
1726–1730	41,400
1731–1735	53,900
1736–1740	58,650

Source: Masson (1911), p.476.

Table 1B.   Woolen Imports from England

Annual Averages in Pieces of Cloth		
	Long Cloth	Short Cloth
1701–1706	19,157	?
1705–1712	17,464	?
1712–1717	16,053	?
1718–1726	14,165	1,890
1727–1740	10,803	1,505.5

Source: Stoianovich (1974), p.77 and Ülker (1974).

The Ottoman Empire's total woolen imports were about 35,000 to 40,000 pieces at the end of the seventeenth century.[18] Imports from France and England already had reached this amount within the first decade of the eighteenth century and after 1736, surpassed it. The total imports from these two countries, together with lesser quantities that were imported from Holland and Venice, make it certain that the first decades of the eighteenth century witnessed a significant expansion in imported woolen textiles. This increase, which should be attributed to the increasing availability of cheap French woolens of middle quality, also meant a significant fall in the overall average price of imported woolens. Indeed, the fall of prices was the most important reason for the accelerated increase in imports over such a short time.

The survival of local woolen manufacturing under such market conditions required strong protectionist state policies as well as entrepreneurs with the ability to take advantage of the most advanced industrial technology and organizational forms of the period.

Contemporary reports make it clear that Ottoman efforts to import technology often encountered active opposition from Western Europeans. The role played by Dessalleurs, the French ambassador in İstanbul, in the 1714 kidnapping and expatriation of a Saxon dyemaster who was one of the technicians brought from Poland, vividly illustrates such attempts to sabotage the Ottoman woolen manufacturing initiative.[19]

The inabililty to obtain technology and the increasingly abundant and cheap manufactured imports made it imperative that the state apply a strictly protectionist regime over the long term. On the one hand, the Ottoman Divan provided every sort of advantage possible in the area of interest-free credit, even long-term capital without repayment. It also helped in securing supplies of raw materials, locating and settling workers, and offering broad tax exemptions. On the other hand, the state's guiding principle of provisionism in no way permitted any form of mercantilistic protectionism, either by curtailing imports, or by imposing duties that would raise domestic prices.

Still another probable cause for the failure of these industries was the inappropriateness of raw materials. The wool produced in the Ottoman Empire generally was not considered suitable for the manufacture of fine-quality woolen textiles.[20] The nature of Ottoman raw material probably played a role, alongside Western European competition, in the decline in quality of Salonica's textile manufactures after the sixteenth century. As a matter of fact, when high-quality woolens once again began to be manufactured in the 1830s, merino sheep were imported since local wool

was considered to be completely inappropriate. And, if we recall that the
rather developed woolen industry of twentieth-century Turkey uses
imported wool, it seems all the more certain that the low quality of raw
materials was a factor in the failure of state manufacturing of woolens in
the eighteenth century.

Silk Manufacture: 1720
Evidence from a number of independent sources makes it clear that
Ottomans consumed more silk cloth than high-quality woolens. Compare,
for example, the woolen and silk cloth consumption by the palace, a major
customer of both types of cloths.

Table 2   Annual Cloth Consumption by the Palace

Year	Woolens		Silk Cloth		Source
	Amount (*Zira*)	Price (*Akçe*)	Amount (*Zira*)	Price (*Akçe*)	
1664	12,468	279	10,685	203	MM.6908
1665	12,380	284	12,111	219	MM.6908
1682	7,019	347	18,537	230	MM.6908, 40
1687	6,019	335	9,375	164	MM.2735, 29
1698	8,884	386	11,348.5	181	MM.2731, 82
1701	9,174	?	11,526	?	MM.429
1750	8,293	?	11,135	?	MM.429

Istanbul, Başbakanlık Arşivi
MM = *Maliyeden Müdevver*

Table 2 makes it clear that, for almost a century, with the exception
of the years 1664 and 1665, the palace obtained more silk than wool cloth.
Moreover, the rich and the notables had similar consumption patterns,
clearly preferring silk cloth throughout the entire eighteenth century. This
impression is confirmed by the composition of the presents distributed by
the *Defterdar* in March 1731. He distributed 5,018 *zira* cloth: only thirteen
percent were woolens and the rest were silks.[21] Also, consider this
assessment, during the 1750s, by a French merchant familiar with
economic conditions in the Middle East: "The silk trade is more important
than that of the woolens. This is because Turks, like the other Levantines,
consume twice as much silk cloth as the woolens."[22] And finally, the
personal expenditure records of a vezir stationed in Belgrade, dated 1785,
show that pure and mixed silk cloths constituted more than eighty percent
of the total of 3,689 *zira* cloth bought.[23]

Silk cloth was also produced in large quantities. While the quality of silk imports, as in the case of woolens, was the highest, the quantity of silk imported was relatively small. Moreover, whereas three to four countries constantly competed in the woolen cloth market, silk cloth imports were dominated by one country—Venice. The fact that Venice, more often than not, was in the enemy camp surely encouraged an import substitution policy. Thus, during the 1717 Ottoman-Venetian war, the palace reduced its purchases of Italian *atlas*, that it normally consumed in large quantities.[24] And in 1720, when the palace decided to establish a silk factory in İstanbul, the stated purpose was: "to produce high quality silk cloth such as *diba*, *hatayî* and *atlas* which are all imported from the Venetian infidel."[25] The task of establishing the factory was given to the palace *bezirgânbaşı*. He found the experts and the machinery among the weavers of the Island of Chios who were flourishing at this period, and capable of producing cloths like those imported from the West. Three craftsmen brought from the island became the chief aides of the *bezirgânbaşı* in founding and later managing the factory.

According to the feasibility report written by these craftsmen, the factory required at least forty looms as well as dyeing, twisting, and final processing facilities in order to produce silk cloth in the desired quality and variety. The fixed capital, excluding the building, was 10,000 *kuruş* and the variable capital, to be utilized after initiation of the production process, was 20,000 *kuruş*. The Divan approved the report and ordered that the 10,000 *kuruş* fixed capital be provided immediately by the Treasury, and the rest be provided as the need arose.[26]

Within a year, twenty-four looms, each with an average cost of 133 *kuruş*, had started to function, the dyehouse was completed and a silk mill "*meşdûd dolabı*" was assembled. These investments cost 4,259 *kuruş*[27] At the weaving and other facilities, forty-four workers were employed. Installation of the brass press (bought for 390 *kuruş* in Chios) at the factory completed the establishment in September 1721. The whole operation took less than a year to complete and cost 8,347.5 *kuruş*, excluding the building.[28]

Each loom was capable of producing 120 to 400 *zira* of cloth per year; since the cost per *zira* would be 34 to 167 *para*, annual production capacity per loom equalled about 300 to 500 *kuruş*. Operating capital per loom, covering the annual wages and the raw material, was estimated at 600 *kuruş*, half was laid out in advance to be reserved to cover the wage payments and the purchase of raw materials for one year.

The factory started production immediately and was granted important privileges and tax exemptions. The three craftsmen who were to organize their lesser subordinates, the *ustabaşı*, *kalfa*, and the *yiğitbaşı*, and another one brought over from Chios to operate the press, worked within a guild-like structure. They were exempted from all the taxes, including *cizye* and *avarız*, and were authorized to carry arms and ride horses, privileges rarely granted to non-Muslims. The same privileges were granted to a "designer" who was employed for the first time in such a factory. There was another, unprecedented, privilege: this was the purchase obligation imposed on government employees. Accordingly, employees were prohibited from purchasing the silk cloth of other domestic and foreign factories as long as the produce of the Chios workers' factory was available. This regulation applied both to government employees in İstanbul and those in the provinces purchasing through their agents in İstanbul.[29]

Under these favorable conditions, the factory expanded its production rapidly and, after satisfying the demand of the palace as well as the bureaucracy, began to supply the free markets beginning in 1723. An order issued by the *Defterdar* deserves attention:

> Weaving of *diba*, *hatayî*, *keneviz*, and *atlas*, which was initiated in the imperial *hatayî* factory, proved to be of finer grade than expected, yet owing to the fact that it is well-known by and in demand among people, not only is most of the materials woven in the abovementioned factory permitted to be sold freely, but also the revenue accruing from their purchase is put to use to replenish the necessary stock of silk and the like and to sustain the continuation of the weaving process. In this manner, if the operation is to be kept on a continual basis...in a short while...the cloth produced there will be circulating throughout the land of Islam. It is apparent that it will be in more demand and more famed than their Venetian namesakes, and since its price is lower than those of similar varieties, it is obvious that everyone will be more than willing to purchase it...

It was decided to rent a shop in the Bedesten whose rent would be paid by the director of the manufacture.

This decision to expose the high quality silk cloths of the state factories to the Venetian competition in the free market reveals a totally new approach in the management of state enterprises. The Ottoman state had always possessed workshops producing for its own needs. Although these workshops sometimes marketed their products in the free market, this practice was unusual except in the case of the so-called fiscal establishments. The sale of state produced commodities such as alum, salt, and the like in the free market aimed at obtaining revenues for the state. But, it must be emphasized, the relationship between the volume and the amount of sales, quality, and cost was not recognized in any of these activities.

The decree opening the silk manufactory to market forces also granted it much needed financial autonomy so that it could be self-sufficient and replenish its capital. From this perspective, we probably are witnessing an antecedent to the state economic enterprises which were to dominate the economy of the Turkish Republic in the twentieth century. It must be noted, however, that this attitude cannot be so clearly observed in the other state enterprises that were established in this period.[30]

Following the beginning of sales in a shop rented in İstanbul, the factory went through an expansionary phase. The number of looms, twenty-four in 1721, increased to fifty-three in three years' time and a second silk mill became operational. With the expansion of capacity, economies of scale were achieved and the average production cost of the main types of silk cloth was reduced by about seven percent. The amount of raw silk inputs increased by twenty percent between 1725 and 1726 (when it stood at 1,600 *okka*—2,000 kg) revealing that the expansion was continuing.[31]

The factory was doing well in the 1730s, when thousands of *ziras* of silk cloths were sent to the shop for sale.[32] Unfortunately, we do not have much information on subsequent developments. There was a devastating fire, after which ten looms were reconstructed in 1756.[33] The latest evidence about the manufactory is from 1760;[34] we surmise that it had lost its importance by then, but might still have continued to function for a couple of more years in order to supply silk cloths for the palace.

In sum, silk cloth manufacture was active for at least forty years for a number of reasons. Not only did it take advantage of the most advanced technology and know-how available locally, but also the strong protectionist policy of the state provided capital and a market. Its withdrawal from the market probably was caused by the stiff competition, not from foreign imports, but, because of mid-eighteenth-century developments in silk manufacturing, from producers all over the empire, especially in İstanbul and Chios. At this time, the Ottoman Empire imported only a small portion of its remarkably vast consumption, and was able to suffice with local manufacture. The state did not attempt to establish or expand state-owned manufacture, but preferred to provide capital for artisanal production. Thus, it was able to guarantee profits from its investments. For example, it provided forty looms with 19,144.5 *kuruş* for the fixed installations of a plant newly constructed in Üsküdar in 1758. The state built the factory and dedicated it as a *vakıf*; it was rented to the artisans who manufactured a newly developing kind of silk cloth known as *yasdik*.

Sail Cloth Manufacture: 1709

The manufacture of sail cloths required for the Ottoman navy was concentrated on the Asian and European coasts of the Aegean Sea, especially at Gallipoli and Çanakkale. The widespread production of these goods in town and city as well as in rural areas met the demands of both the navy and the civilian fleets and was sufficent even for exportation.[35]

The number of large sailing vessels and the galleons used by the Ottoman navy increased to some thirty-five to forty by the early eighteenth century.[36] The increasing number of large vessels necessitated more, and better made, firm and heavy sail cloths. The organization and capacity of the existing artisanal manufacture, intended to meet the demands of the medium and small tonnage vessels, did not have the capability of adapting to the changing requirements, either in quantity or quality. Moreover, the Ottoman state's purchasing policy did not encourage such a flexibility; indeed it made it more difficult. According to this policy known as *mirî mübayaa*, the state, by imposing a levy-like taxation, purchased sailcloths at a fixed price below the market price, sometimes even below the production cost. When state demands were only a small portion of the production, the producers offset the loss with profits made in selling their products at normal prices in the market. But when state demands were heavy, their losses were great. The rigidity of the Ottoman financial system and the *mirî mübayaa* policy did not allow price increases in the market in response to increased demand. Therefore, when state demands increased, producers usually reacted by decreasing either the quality or the quantity of production. When the state set new standards, its supply became more difficult. Hence, the first imports of sailcloths.[37]

By 1709, the manufacture of sail cloths was established in the Arsenal at İstanbul in an effort to meet the demand for more and better quality products. In the state-owned physical plant, the organization of production was assigned to an entrepreneur. This *bezcibaşı*, the director who managed the manufacture, was obliged to provide the navy with a certain amount of sailcloths every year. The state provided a sample that set the standard for the sailcloths to be produced. The *bezcibaşı* would buy cotton yarns from the dealers in İstanbul, at a price bound by contract, and he would collect the total amount in cash from the Treasury at the beginning of each year. He would be paid at a fixed price—2 *akçe* for each *zira* manufactured—and would receive that sum also at the beginning of each year. Thus the *bezcibaşı* would be acting like a subcontractor; he would organize the workers and pay their wages. The enterprise was to provide 30,000 *zira* of sailcloth per year, twenty-five to thirty percent of total navy needs during times of peace. During wartime, the production would increase up to 200,000 *zira*, forty to fifty percent of the total requirements.[38] In this way, difficulties arising from increased demands imposed on private producers would be eliminated. At the same time, the real purpose of the new policy was to secure a channel for the steady supply of high quality sailcloths.

The manufactory was designed to accommodate the increased demand that occurred during wartime. When at peace, the *bezcibaşı*, instead of decreasing production, was permitted to sell the surplus in the free market to civilians. But, in wartime conditions such as in 1713, when production increased sharply as war drew near, sales to the civilians were forbidden.[39]

By the end of the war of 1714–1718, the production of sailcloths for the navy was reduced (to 30,000 *zira*) and the ban on private production was removed. But the very high-quality and expensive sailcloth had little appeal in the civilian economy, and so the number of looms fell from about thirty or forty to ten by 1750.[40]

The *bezcibaşı* then appealed to the Divan. Claiming that the annual needs of the navy for 30,000 *zira* sailcloth could not be met by so few looms, he asked that the private looms in İstanbul participate in the production. If the private looms, then numbering twenty-four, were not willing to do so, their production should be stopped and the *bezcibaşı*'s monopoly restored. He proposed this as the only way to meet the demand of the navy.[41] Accepting the petition of the *bezcibaşı*, the Divan asked the thirty-four loom owners (ten state-owned and twenty-four private) to produce 900 *zira* sailcloth each at a fixed price to meet the total demand of 30,000 *zira*. But the production cost was twenty-four *akçe*, and the Divan offered seventeen *akçe* per *zira*—some thirty percent less. Since each loom would lose 6,300 *akçe* every year, private loom owners refused. Consequently, according to the *bezcibaşı's* proposal, private production was banned (ca.1751), and the monopoly of sailcloth production was reestablished in İstanbul and environs. Two years later, the monopoly was extended to include İzmir.[42]

Manufacture thus was revitalized and, by 1760, once again reached full capacity.[43] When demand increased during the war with Russia (1768–1774), the existing capacity expanded in 1770 by new establishments.[44] After the war was over, the demand of the navy increased even more. Not only did the navy rebuild, making up for its losses during the war, but it also became more active against Russian naval forces in the Black Sea, no longer, after 1774, an Ottoman lake. Annual demand for sail cloths increased, at a minimum, to 60,000 *zira* by 1777.[45] Actual demand, which fluctuated according to immediate needs, was much above this figure.

Table 3   Sailcloth Required by the Navy

Years	Amount
1774	140,000
1777	222,000
1781	118,000
1782	196,000
1783	182,635
1791	160,000
1801	200,000
1802	250,000
1803	300,000

Sources: İstanbul, Başbakanlık Arşivi, MM.19549, pp.13–24; TKSA.E.9572; MM.10405, p.178; Cevdet Bahriye (C. Bah.) 10325; C.Bah.217; C.Bah.3326; MM.9997, pp.428–429.

In order to meet these rapidly increasing demands of the navy, sailcloth manufacture grew in capacity and the number of looms reached fifty by 1785.[46] The rapid growth in demand, not only triggered increases in capacity, but also, paradoxically, hindered its growth. The increase in capacity could never catch up with demand. Behind this paradoxical relationship was the distribution of wages and market relations. On the one hand, what the navy paid for the sailcloth was below its production cost. However, since the wages were paid in advance by the beginning of each year, the manufactory was able to accumulate capital in the form of credit. The *bezcibaşı* sold a considerable amount of the sailcloths manufactured by using this capital in the free market and delaying the delivery of goods to the navy until the end of the year. Thus, he made some profit and expanded activities at the manufactory. This was the case between 1750 and 1760 when he was able to sell in the free market under the monopoly regulations. Yet after 1769, when the navy increased its demand rapidly and started to buy all of the production, the chances of selling in the free market were reduced and the manufactory incurred losses. For example, in 1776, the Arsenal lost 2,448 kuruş keeping the contract to supply sailcloth to the navy, but made 600 kuruş profit from sales in the free market.[47] The *bezcibaşı* was obliged to put up his own house as security in order to continue production.[48] In response, the Divan increased the unit price paid for the sailcloth, bringing it closer to production costs. With advance payment, the manufactory was able to make some profit and to continue production.

This depended on the ready availability of cotton yarn, which constituted eighty percent of the production cost, at a stable price. One of the reasons for establishing a monopoly in sailcloth manufacture in 1750 was to stabilize cotton yarn prices at a reasonable rate by reducing the demand of the private producers. In the second half of the eighteenth century, maintenance of such stability became increasingly difficult because of the inflation that resulted from the new monetary regulations. Moreover, the price of cotton yarn began to increase more rapidly than inflation because of a number of factors, these included: increased demand for Ottoman cotton yarn in Central Europe; the war in the Aegean Sea, which interrupted maritime transportation; and, factors such as piracy and plague, which reduced supplies, especially in İstanbul. With its limited resources, the Treasury could not sufficiently adapt to the increase. As a result, sailcloth manufacture continuously suffered losses and could not meet the demand of the navy.

The precautions taken against this situation typify Ottoman economic behavior; cotton yarn was incorporated within the policy of *mirî mübayaa* by the end of the eighteenth century. State officials directly bought the yarn needed for sailcloth manufacture from the western Anatolian production centers. At first, producers managed to supply some ten tons of cotton yarn required by the state. When the demand increased, they reduced the quantity and the quality of the cotton yarn as they often did with other products and services regulated also by the *mirî mübayaa*. Feeling the impact of technologically more advanced Western products, Ottoman cotton yarn producers, who already were suffering from a shrinking market, refrained from selling their products in this period of inflation when the state offered prices that did not change for years and remained very low. Thus, sailcloth production was reduced by the shortage of cotton yarn and the navy was obliged to rely on imports (mostly from Russia).

To avoid imports, the Divan decided to establish a spinning mill in İstanbul.[49] It was founded in November 1826 with capital derived from the pious foundations. There were fourteen animal-powered machines, modeled on English prototypes and made by local craftsmen. The machines busied 114 workers and had 1,680 spindles with a daily capacity of 225 kilograms cotton yarn.[50] With the addition of this spinning mill, the manufacture of sailcloth became the first integrated cotton industry in Ottoman Turkey. Its total capacity of 250,000 *zira* was intended solely for the navy, and sales in the free market were banned.[51]

The manufacture of sailcloth was the most enduring of the industries established with state capital. Several factors contributed to its endurance over the course of the century. First, there was never any difficulty in providing technology or qualified workers in this traditional branch of textile industry. Second, the navy provided a secure and continuous demand even though wages were very low. But payment of the wages in advance, at the beginning of each year, offset their low level; thus, when capital was scarce and expensive, this policy provided secure credit. Third, a manager who had a personal stake in the enterprise not salaried bureaucrats contributed to its capacity to sell in the market under monopoly regulations. The possible relationship between its disappearance in mid-nineteenth century and the ban on the sales in free market are interesting topics that require investigation.

NOTES

1. Genç (1987a).

2. Genç (1987b), 156.

3. The *malikâne*-owners, most of whom were members of the military class, were not guaranteed property rights and therefore realized the above-mentioned investments only within the *vakıf* system.

4. Svoronos (1956), 245, Beaujour (1800) I, 72–75. The comparison of these figures regarding the cotton production in Macedonia, which constitutes only a small portion of cotton production and consumption in

the Ottoman Empire, with the figures from England, the seat of the "Industrial Revolution", bring out very interesting results. England consumed 4.2 million lbs. in 1772 and 15.5 million lbs. in 1792. In 1790, the Salonica-Macedonia region alone spun 7 million lbs. of cotton into yarn and used half of it in weaving. Başbakanlık Arşivi (İstanbul) Maliyeden Müdevver (hereafter MM) 9957, 15 (1743–47), 67 (1751); Cevdet İktisat (hereafter C.I.) 1137 (1790–1801); MM 8567, 122–123 (1820).

5. MM 10178, 195 (1735); MM 10203, 193 (1760).

6. Braude (1979).

7. The other was the sailcloth factory; although sailcloth was not an imported item, the factory was established to create a potential of supply in appropriate amounts, quality, and time.

8. Svoronos (1956), 256.

9. Braude (1979).

10. de Peysonnel (1787), I, 57–58.

11. Stoianovich (1974), 86, 91.

12. "*kefere memleketinden gelen çukadan müstagni olmak mülahazası ile.*" Topkapı Sarayı Müzesi Arşivi (İstanbul) (hereafter TKSA) E. 6074.

13. Svoronos (1956), 255.

14. MM 2488, 118.

15. Varenbergh (1874), 326.

16. MM 7560, 298.

17. MM 7560, 303.

18. Stoianovich (1974), 80.

19. Stoianovich (1974), 91.

20. Svoronos (1956), 240.

21. MM 10172, 12ff.

22. Flachat (1765), 287.

23. Başbakanlık Arşivi Kamil Kepeci (İstanbul) (hereafter KK) 791.

24. Başbakanlık Arşivi (İstanbul) Başmuhasebe Defterleri (hereafter D.BŞM), 1129.4.29, April 12th, 1717.

25. KK707, 43/72 1135, 8.9.1723.

26. KK 706, 38.

27. KK 706, 29–31 and 39.

28. MM 1736, 250 and D.BŞM. 1443.

29 KK 706, 49/29 B 1142,28.2.1729.

30. The sailcloth manufactory, established in 1709 (and examined later in this article), also competed in the free market, but it did not assume the mercantile attitude so clearly evident in the case of the silk factory.

31. KK 706, 44 (İbnülemin-Muafiyet/İmtiyazat no:140).

32. D.BŞM. 1689/1732–1735.

33. MM 8947, 551.

34. TKSA.E.6074.

35. France, Ministère des Affaires Étrangères Paris (hereafter Aff. Étr.) Biii239, no: 14.

36. MM 2483, 127–133 and C. Bah. 8814.

37. MM 10149, 124, 1703.

38. MM 10309, 155; MM 6266, 138 and Genç (1984), 90.

39. MM 9983, 281.

40. MM 9983, 282.

41. The daily production of one single loom was around fifteen *zira* (C.Bah. 12404 and MM 10309, 55) and, in one year, it was possible to have 30,000 *zira* woven in ten looms. However, the fixed price—2 *akçe* per each *zira*—that the state had paid since 1709 was inadequate. Wages had risen by fifty percent between 1709–1750. Thus, the private sector would have endured considerable losses.

42. MM 9983, 282–283; MM 9976, 270.

43. MM 8947, 672.

44. MM 10381, 157.

45. C.Bah. 12251.

46. C.Bah. 9466.

47. C.Bah. 10485.

48. *"evini rehin bırakmak zorunda"* C.Bah. 12251.

49. MM 8958, 219.

50. MM 8882, 160–161.

51. MM 8882, 154.

REFERENCES CITED

Başbakanlık Arşivi (İstanbul)
        Maliyeden Müdevver
        Cevdet Bahriye
        Cevdet İktisat
        Kamil Kepeci
        Başmuhasebe Defterleri
Topkapı Sarayı Müzesi Arşivi (Istanbul)

Beaujour, Felix de
    1800   *Tableau du commerce de la Grèce*, Paris (English translation: *A View of the Commerce of Greece*. London).

Braude, Benjamin
    1979   "International Competition and Domestic Cloth in the Ottoman Empire, 1500–1650," *Review*, II.3.

Flachat, Jean-Claude
    1765   *Observations sur le commerce et sur les arts d'une partie de l'Europe, de l'Asie, de l'Afrique, et même des Indes Orientales.* Lyon.

France, Ministère de Affaires Étrangères (Paris).
        Biii 239

Genç, Mehmet
    1984   "XVIII. yüzyılda Osmanlı ekonomisi ve savaş," *Yapıt*.

Genç, Mehmet
    1987a   "Entreprises d'état et attitude politique dans l'industrie
             ottomane au XVIIIe siècle," Jacques Thobie and Jean-Louis
             Bacqué Grammont, eds., *L'accession de la Turquie à la
             civilisation industrielle. Facteurs internes et externes,*
             İstanbul.

Genç, Mehmet
    1987b   "17–19. yüzyıllarda sanayi ve ticaret merkezi olarak Tokat,"
             *Türk tarihinde ve kültüründe Tokat Sempozyumu, 2–6
             Temmuz 1986.* Ankara.

Issawi, Charles
    1988   *The Fertile Crescent 1800–1914. A Documentary Eco-
             nomic History.* New York.

Masson, Paul
             *Histoire du commerce français dans le Levant au XVIIIe
             siècle.* Paris.

Peysonnel, Ch. de
    1787   *Traité du commerce dans la mer Noire,* vol. 2, Paris.

Stoianovich, Troian
    1974   "Pour un modèle du commerce du Levant: économie
             concurrentielle et économie de bazar, 1500–1800," *Bulletin
             d'Association Internationale d'Études Sud-est Européennes,*
             XII.

Svoronos, Nicholas
    1956   *Le commerce de Salonique au XVIII siècle.* Paris.

Ülker, Necmi
    1974   "The Rise of İzmir, 1688–1740," Ph.d. dissertation,
             University of Michigan, Ann Arbor.

Varenbergh, Emile
    1874   *Histoire des relations diplomatiques entre le comte de
             Flandre et l'Angleterre au moyen age.* Brussels.

von Scherzer, K.
    1873   *Smyrna,* Wein.

4

Ottoman Manufacturing in the Nineteenth Century*

Donald Quataert

In writing the story of nineteenth-century Ottoman manufacturing, historians have focused on its decline in the face of European competition. This article takes a different view. Using textile manufacturing as the example, it makes clear that the fate of late Ottoman industry is more complicated and interesting than flat assertions of decline have suggested. Some textile industries permanently did diminish over the period, particularly those that had been competing in the international market. Others, however, only temporarily lost customers during the first onslaught of European imports, ca. 1820–1850, but then regained them after adjusting to the new conditions. Overall, there was a marked manufacturing revival, beginning in the early 1870s and continuing, with fluctuations, until World War I.

This upward shift derived from a mix of international and local factors. Among the most directly relevant international factors were the ongoing mechanization of yarn spinning and cloth weaving in Europe and the United States as well as the development of factory-made dyestuffs. We also should include the rising disparity of wealth between the Middle

---

*This article is a greatly condensed version of material found in Quataert (1993b).

East and the West and the latter's shift to capital equipment production. Domestic factors include a shrinking empire with a rising population and the local presence of abundant raw materials.

Later in the period, the international price depression of 1873–1896 reduced Ottoman cultivators' buying power, making imports relatively more expensive. Ottoman manufacturing expanded in the breech, using a mix of cost-cutting imported technologies, reduced wages, and paying careful attention to local tastes.

During the post-1873 period, imports of European goods continued to mount, although less impressively than before. Since both indigenous production and imports of foreign manufactures increased in tandem, total Ottoman consumption rose by the sum of two. The Ottoman population also was increasing at this time, a function of natural causes and the immigration of millions of Muslims from Russia. We can approximate the size of the population increase but the precise value or volume of Ottoman consumption of manufactured goods remains unknown since only the import statistics are available. Thus, the important question of per capita consumption remains open although some increase is certain.[1]

The Ottoman lands generally possessed abundant supplies of raw materials, both raw cotton and wool as well as dyestuffs. In the 1850s, for example, Asia Minor altogether produced about 50,000 bales of cotton while Macedonia produced 1.5 million okkes and Thessaly another 500 to 600,000 okkes.[2] In the early twentieth century, the regions of Adana, Syria, and west Anatolia yielded some 80,000 bales of raw cotton.[3]

Dyestuffs generally derived from local sources, the most important of these being madder root, the source of the famed "Turkey-red" color so valued by European and Ottoman consumers, and yellow berries as well. The development of artificial dyes during the 1850s and 1860s, first in England and then Germany, transformed the Ottoman textile industry. Despite problems with improper use and sometimes with color fastness, these new materials freed Middle East textile producers from the often laborious task of gathering and preparing natural dyestuffs, or paying others for the work, while also liberating them from the vagaries of nature. The new dyes enabled them to color their yarns and cloths with very inexpensive materials that, compared to the natural substances, were simple to apply. Textile makers now could bypass professional dyehouses, at some risk to quality and fastness but with considerable savings.[4]

Adoption of the new dyestuffs varied considerably according to region and producers applied them both to locally-made and imported yarn. It was not always a trend of abandoning local dyes for synthetics. Sometimes manufacturers quit and then resumed local dyeing in their efforts to find the most marketable combination of product and price. In the 1880s, for example, Aleppo producers started buying large quantities of aniline and alizarin dyes to undercut their competitors. But, after losing customers, they resumed colored yarn imports. By contrast, competitors at Aintab bought a recently developed and cheap synthetic dye for its lower-end textiles, while importing dyed yarns for the better qualities.[5] Several important textile production centers continued to dye locally, while others imported their colored yarn needs. In Mardin district ca. 1900, for example, local dyers colored virtually all of the yarn imported while at Maraş, less than one-half of all yarn imported was dyed.[6] Trabzon producers at this time imported substantial quantities of cochineal, indigo, campeche, and alizarin to dye cotton yarn but imported colored yarns for better quality and specialized goods and for colors the local dyers couldn't provide.[7] Dyers at the important textile center of Tokat then were importing red yarns from Switzerland and Germany but otherwise colored imported yarn, imparting a fastness considered more durable than the European colors.[8] Until the opening of yarn-dyeing factories late in the nineteenth century, İzmir area users employed important quantities of vegetable dyes.[9]

The following contribution is divided into two sections of quite unequal length. The first and larger section treats textile production for the domestic Ottoman market. In some cases, the manufacturers and their customers lived in the same district or province while, in other instances, at considerable distances from one another, in different provinces and regions and sometimes, on different continents. To some extent, the length of this section is greater because the story of Middle East production for internal markets is not well known. The second reason, however, is simply that production for the domestic market is the central story of nineteenth-century Ottoman industry. Indeed, the argument that nine-teenth-century Ottoman manufacturing declined has gone unchallenged because, in large part, production for the domestic market was not taken into consideration. The decline paradigm fed upon the failure of many Ottoman export industries to continue competing in the changing market conditions of the age.

The number of industries focused on international exports surely fell after 1800. But several new ones emerged and these form the subject of our second section. The export industries shared with many domestically targeted sectors a reliance on cheap labor, that generally suffered a decline

in real wages. More exceptionally, these export industries employed girls
and women in disproportionately high numbers, compared to their participation in the domestically oriented sectors. The presence of female
labor in manufacturing was commonplace in the nineteenth century and
before, but the size of females' role in export production is striking. These
female workers were among the very worst paid in the Ottoman industrial
workforce. Here then, we clearly see the terms under which Ottoman
producers participated in the international economy.

WHY THE COMPARATIVE LACK OF MECHANIZED FACTORIES IN THE OTTOMAN EMPIRE?

This study primarily focuses on the vibrancy of hand manufacturing
in the nineteenth-century Ottoman Middle East although machine-based
production is discussed. Textiles are its main subject because this is where
the sources led. Although industries such as food processing and leather-
making were important, they received scant attention in the wide range of
Ottoman and European sources, both primary and secondary, consulted
for this study.

The intent here is to find out what did occur in Ottoman manufacturing, not to explain why an Ottoman industrial revolution never
developed. Such an explanation, it seems, would lead to a sterile
conclusion that the Middle East, during the nineteenth century, did not
follow the Western path of development. Since no country outside the
West did so, except for Japan, this approach does not seem fruitful.
Therefore, the following will only touch on the long list of factors
impeding Ottoman development of a Manchester-style industrial
infrastructure.[10]

Foreigners were fond of blaming government corruption, in-
efficiency and ineptitude for the underdevelopment of Ottoman
manufacturing during the nineteenth century, by which they meant the
general absence of mechanized factories. There were plenty of Ottoman
laws promoting industrialization although most of these came quite late,
after 1870. These often remained dead letter; tax exemptions, for example,
were without effect when customs officials collected the duties anyway.[11]
Laws providing for duty-free import of all machines installed in a new
factory had been on the books since 1873, and were renewed regularly
thereafter. In addition, orders from 1876 freed Ottoman industrial
products from both internal and external customs duties.[12] Some historians
have pointed to the apparent correlation between the various enactments

of duty-free legislation and the bursts of factory founding that did occur.[13] In this analysis, by implication, Ottoman industrialization would have been more successful if only government legislation had been more enlightened and consistent.

Two brief comments seem appropriate here. First, it is true that government policy focused on agriculture rather than manufacturing. But the assumption that such a comparative lack of emphasis on industrial development spelled the presence of a backward, unenlightened government is unfair. Rather, we need to consider that segments of the bureaucracy perceived that there were advantages in having cheap industrial imports. Powerful policy-making elements did not favor import substitution policies. This is a perfectly rational option. In common with most of the world outside of nineteenth-century Europe and the United States (and Japan), "neither markets nor input supplies were attractive and therefore it was more profitable to supply manufactured goods from outside than to make them in the country concerned."[14] Overall, the steady fall in the price of manufactured goods and, for much of the period except 1873–1896, the reverse pattern for agricultural commodities, pushed Ottoman entrepreneurs and workers towards the agrarian sector at the expense of the industrial. Second, the role of state policy has been vastly exaggerated by both contemporary observers during the nineteenth century and my colleagues in Ottoman history. While state policy certainly was significant, its importance was not unlimited. The eight percent internal duty on goods shipped from one point to another certainly did hurt factory owners who were trying to establish broad internal markets.[15] But, government policy was not the critical factor in the formation of Ottoman cotton yarn factories, or for that matter, the general pace and tempo of Ottoman industrialization.

Rather, we should look at the host of other factors that severely circumscribed policy-making options. In the realm of politics, we need to remember that Britain was the dominant power until the 1870s, and actively sought to prevent the development of rival manufacturers. When Britain, in the 1830s, destroyed Mohammed Ali Pasha, the Egyptian dynasty builder, the lesson was made clear. He had been pursuing industrialization in order to develop his power base in Egypt and the British quite deliberately dismantled his considerable accomplishments to remove the threat to their Middle Eastern markets. Instead, Britain during its industrial hegemony sought to permit only free trade. From the perspective of international politics, Ottoman industrial development was not a viable option for İstanbul planners.

The absence of security in the early years of the nineteenth century certainly discouraged the large capital investment needed for a factory and all its equipment, so readily visible and subject to predation by bandits and marauders. The lack of water resources certainly was critical in many areas. It should be recalled that water power played a crucial role in early American and European manufacturing and steam did not replace water power until late in the nineteenth century. This water option simply was not available in most of the Ottoman world.

The comparative sparseness of the Ottoman population depressed manufacturing potential as well. Relatively low population densities, in the absence of countervailing factors, meant an overall shortage of workers that discouraged the massing of labor power so necessary to factory life. Not coincidentally, most factories emerged in the relatively more densely populated areas such as the European provinces, İstanbul and İzmir. Low densities also reduced the possibilities for labor-intensive industrial activities, although these were present. Also, the population of twenty-six million was very thinly scattered over the territorially vast Ottoman Empire. Nor was the total potential market terribly large; compare, for example, the Ottoman population to that of contemporary Qing China, that held some 350 million persons. And finally, the small and scattered Ottoman population and its proximity to Europe made Ottoman manufacturing more vulnerable to Western interference than its Chinese contemporary.[16]

Factory formation, moreover, was retarded by the actions of the Ottoman populace; Ottoman workers, entrepreneurs, and the population at large, passively and actively resisted the formation of many factories. Elite groups including state officials participated, at least sometimes. There was considerable publicly expressed concern, for example, about the air and water pollution that a factory might bring. Such objections have a face value but they surely camouflaged the fear of economic competition as well. In 1875, for example, entrepreneurs sought to found a water-powered yarn factory in the town of Niaousta. The Salonica provincial administrative council, that had jurisdiction, carefully stated the conditions under which the factory could be built. In particular, it would not be permitted to interfere with the livelihoods of town dwellers. Because women had been producing wool yarn in workshops of the town since olden times, the factory therefore could produce only cotton yarn. Nor could the factory diminish the water supplies needed for the local gardens, orchards, and fields.[17] There was a similar popular and official response when a British subject opened an İzmir factory for printing muslin. Some local Armenian manufacturers, whose factory offered a similar product, protested and İstanbul consequently ordered the new factory to close.[18] Sometimes the evidence of resistance is unclear. On a number of occasions, a newly opened factory caught fire and was destroyed. Was this active resistance, or merely the result of carelessness or the hazards of the age? For example, a fez factory, built in Salonica in 1908–9, burned down almost immediately and was not rebuilt.[19] At Trabzon, a British firm bought and imported the machinery for a cotton and woolen weaving plant "but while in store a fire damaged them greatly so that most of the parts will have to be renewed."[20] Other known examples of resistance include that of Uşak where, in the early 1890s, two capitalists tried to erect a wool spinning factory for carpet making. In the face of strong protests from local residents who feared the loss of hand spinning jobs, the government denied the concession. Wool yarn factories later were built at Uşak anyway, only to be sacked and burned by angry hand spinners in March 1908.[21] But they did reopen. At Adana, a knitting factory "was burnt down and never started again."[22] Resistance, that included factory burning, however, did not prevent the emergence of a major cluster of steam-powered factories, to reel silk, in the Bursa district during the 1850s. Nor can we trace the general absence of factories to Ottoman machine breakers, however fascinating they were.

PRODUCTION FOR DOMESTIC OTTOMAN MARKETS

Yarn Production

Ottoman cotton yarn producers labored in a context of (nearly) steadily falling yarn prices throughout the nineteenth century. During the late eighteenth and early nineteenth centuries, Indian and Ottoman yarns lost out to British goods. Thereafter, for most of the century, England nearly totally dominated the import of unbleached yarns while, for a time, Belgium supplied most of the balance. Thanks to lower labor and transport costs, the Italian producers, near the end of the century, drove out the Belgians. Indian spinners (re)entered the Ottoman market at about the same time, underselling the British and competing with the Italians. By 1914, India provided as much as twenty percent of all Ottoman yarn imports.[23]

Toward the end of the century, a number of mechanized Ottoman spinning mills emerged, employing very cheap female and child labor. The founding of cotton yarn factories occurred at two distinctively different periods. The first group emerged during the 1870s and 1880s while the second cluster of factory foundings occurred after 1896. There were a few mills at widely scattered locations. The earliest privately owned yarn factory probably was at Harput, established ca. 1864.[24] Others were located at Elazığ, in ca. 1903, and at Gallipoli, founded before 1913. The vast majority of Ottoman yarn factories were located in just a few areas, notably İzmir, Adana, Salonica and, to a lesser extent, İstanbul. At the beginning of the twentieth century, Ottoman mills provided some thirteen percent of all mechanically spun yarn used within the empire; within a decade, their share had reached about one-quarter of the total.[25] Thus, by the period's end, Ottoman suppliers of machine-made cotton yarn were competing with British, Belgian, Italian, and Indian producers.

Amidst the price-cutting wars of these machine producers, the manual spinning of yarn both by wheel and by hand persisted in many districts. In the late eighteenth century, these hand-producers of Ottoman yarn had been locked in a struggle with Indian and European, mainly Dutch, suppliers. Ottoman yarn producers then were still important exporters. From around Serez, Salonica, and Thessaly, for example, they shipped substantial quantities of yarn abroad. North Anatolian yarn spinners exported massive quantities to the Crimea while İzmir shipped important amounts to Marseilles.[26]

During the first half of the nineteenth century, the yarn was produced through a variety of organizational forms that differed in the many cities, towns, and villages of its origin. Free labor spun the yarn in thousands of village homes, often for family use or casual sale in nearby markets. In addition, merchants organized substantial putting-out systems, involving large numbers of village and town spinners. Kayseri merchants were operating a very widespread network, buying raw cotton from Adana (some seventy percent of its total output) and distributing it to spinners throughout central and northern Anatolia. In some cities, guilds provided the yarn. Labor of various kinds made yarn in government workshops. In the Eyüp quarter of İstanbul, for example, about sixty non-Muslims spun in a state-run factory, rewarded by exemption from the poll tax (and perhaps cash payments as well).[27] State factories regularly employed several hundreds of orphaned children to spin yarn for the Ottoman fleet. The children were "suitably paid" and worked in the factories for short, specified periods of time, on a rotational basis. In the 1850s, these used persons convicted of misdemeanor offenses, who worked off their sentences and were released. Others spun under government orders, e.g. those on the Gallipoli peninsula who received piecework wages to supply yarn to the tentmakers' guild in İstanbul.[28]

Beginning in ca. 1790, English machine-made yarn started to substantially underprice the Ottoman and Indian products, thanks to steampower and exploitative, labor-intensive employment practices. The Ottoman import of machine-made yarn increased by leaps and bounds and, in a mere three decades, had risen tenfold.[29] Nineteenth-century Ottoman yarn production probably reached its nadir in ca. 1870.[30] Ottoman hand spinning was abandoned, rapidly and permanently, in some areas. At some places, such as the famed town of Ambelakia in Thessaly, the Ottoman export trade in yarn evaporated immediately and the decaying town became a symbol for the decline of Ottoman industry.

The replacement of British- for Ottoman-made yarn, however, was not an automatic or uniform process; rather it occurred with considerable variations in timing and extent. More surprisingly, the manual spinning of Ottoman yarn in significant quantities persisted. Geography played some role but was a less important variable than has been assumed.[31] Other factors were more important, such as poverty and the existence of putting-out networks.[32] Rural households, generally, were slower to accept the imports than town or city textile manufacturers. The availability of alternative manufacturing and/or agricultural opportunities certainly promoted the shift from locally- to foreign-made yarn.

In some areas, the adoption of British yarn was completed or well advanced by the mid 1830s, for example, at the textile-producing centers of Tokat and Yozgat as well as at Arapkir, where yarn imports gave birth to a new weaving industry (discussed later).[33] Residents of the Bursa region were among the first to switch to British yarn because they had a ready and familiar alternative activity to turn to, silk spinning. At this critical transition time, silk spinning was not the ill-paying activity that it became somewhat later. In the 1830s, it offered high wages to attract badly needed workers (discussed later).

The use of Ottoman homespun, however, continued. In some areas, its use persisted for only a few decades more than in locations where British yarn immediately had been adopted. Elsewhere, hand spinning was present until the end of the Ottoman Empire. Much of the surviving spinning industry rested in the hands of rural women who spun for their own needs and sold the surplus for example, those of the Niğde and Aleppo areas. Around Kayseri, cotton and wool spinning remained an everyday part of women's skills until World War I.[34]

Commercial weavers used hand spun yarn, in combination with factory yarns, to produce cloths of a desired strength, fineness, and price. Women spinning at home in Sivas province during the early 1890s used spinning wheels to produce commercial yarn for a coarse cloth used in men's trousers.[35] By 1907, however, yarn made in Adana factories was employed more usually.[36] Weavers in Aleppo ca. 1900 still used regionally spun yarn for the warp thread in many of the coarser textiles. Women working at home spun an estimated 100,000 kg/year.[37]

Yarn spinning in the districts surrounding Diyarbakır retained great vitality among the Kurdish tribal population who depended on the income it produced. In ca. 1907, for example, Mardin district spinners provided local weavers with an estimated 45,000 kg for use in the warp.[38] At Harput, ca. 1900, villagers hand carded over 700,000 kg of raw cotton and spun it on small wheels for use on home looms. Unlike weavers in Sivas province and at Aleppo who used hand-spun for the warp, Harput weavers employed it for the weft (and for candle wicks).[39]

Handspinning survived in part because some could not afford to purchase any yarn at any price. Also, many families did not give monetary value to the time the women spent spinning, counting as net savings the sums not spent to purchase yarns. But much of the surviving spinning was aimed at the market. These spinners were able to continue working because their yarn undersold the European product. It was not yarn of comparable quality but yarn of the coarsest kind, that nonetheless had a wide variety of uses. Since the prices of imported yarn and cloth fell steadily over the century, so too, surely, did the prices of local handspun yarn, and the wages of the spinners.

In the final quarter of the century, Ottoman hand spinners encountered new competitors—mechanized Ottoman yarn mills—while continuing their battle with the foreign producers. These new mills spun yarn in a wide range of numbers but focused on the lower numbers, precisely the coarser yarns that had become the handspinners' last refuge. By the turn of the century, in a context of increasingly intense international competition and falling yarn prices, matters had become very grim for the Ottoman hand spinners.

Cloth Production

The Ottoman manufacture of cloth retained a strong vitality during the nineteenth century despite falling textile prices, changing technologies and fashions and severe foreign competition. Overall, there was a major shift in favor of cotton textiles, at the expense of other materials. Among the workers and peasants, the use of home-spun cotton yarn declined as did their consumption of wool, animal skins, and mohair. The use of mohair cloth vanished almost entirely. Among the Ottoman upper classes, cotton largely replaced silk and mohair as the fabric of choice. As cotton cloth usage rose to the first rank, some other textiles hung on; linen cloth use in fact rose over time. Similarly, the use of silk and silk-cotton cloth persisted for much of the century and then significantly increased, on a per capita basis, towards its end.[40]

Ottoman imports of cotton cloth grew enormously over the century. They annually averaged 450 tons during the early 1820s and 4,100 tons just two decades later. Astonishing increases continued, to 17,000 tons/year in the early 1870s and finally, to 49,000 tons between 1909–1911.[41] British producers always dominated the overall textile import market but, i.a., the Swiss, Germans, French and Austrians offered greater and lesser competition over the century in certain textiles and market segments.

Ottoman cloth manufacturers survived by employing several kinds of strategies, notably price reductions. Hence they adopted factory-made yarns and dyes and cut wages through the abandonment of guild in favor of rural and household labor. Machine-made yarn (European as well as Ottoman later on) offered price, quality, and regularity advantages. At the same time, as seen, producers continued to use homespun yarns alone or in combination with machine-made for certain textiles because of the texture and cheaper price. Ottoman weavers frequently focused on making the non-Western clothing still beloved by so many of their customers. Here, the producers both encouraged the maintenance of unique local fashions and created new ones as well.

The wearing of "traditional" clothing—here only meaning non-Western—by both men and women of all communities, remained very common. This is true despite the ongoing westernization of the region's inhabitants. Much of the imported cloth, it turns out, was not modern and Western in design but rather European imitations of Middle Eastern patterns and styles. Some patterns were hardly of long-standing usage. Ottoman merchants had invented them, trying to keep their European competitors off balance by rapidly changing fashions and creating patterns difficult to replicate in a factory. It was not, I should add, only that producers found refuge in weaving and dyeing particular cloths in the small quantities that were not worthy of European manufacturers' attentions or that they underbid them for the bottom of the market.[42] Ottoman producers sometimes did survive because of the tiny niche in the market they filled or because they produced the coarsest textiles at extremely low prices. But these are not adequate explanations. Ottoman manufacturers often out-competed the Europeans for products that sold in extremely large quantities, winning because they knew their customers' needs better. Also, the Ottoman product was slightly more expensive and won favor because of durability and style, not price.

Wool cloth production remained important in several areas during the nineteenth century, notably around Salonica in the southeastern Balkans and in east-central Anatolia. Both regions were centers of sheep raising, affording easily accessible sources of the raw material. Early in the century, the famed Jewish wool cloth makers in the city of Salonica supplied the Janissary Corps with wool cloth uniforms and exported goods to Italy and France. In the surrounding countryside, villagers wove large quantities of wool cloth for shipment to İzmir and western Europe. By the mid-century mark, however, English and continental wool weavers had driven Salonica cloth from these markets just as the 1826 destruction of the Janissary Corps eliminated this important domestic market. Thus, the urban-based wool cloth industry at Salonica went into eclipse for most of the century.[43]

But Salonica province retained considerable importance as a producer of textiles for the domestic Ottoman market. And, beginning in the late 1880s, with the emergence of local spinning mills, the region substantially increased cloth production. The weaving of coarse wool cloth remained important in the rural areas around Salonica and in the Macedonian countryside. Three of the leading coarse wool cloth centers, the Nevrokop, Niaousta, and Mayada regions, contained some 2,125 looms during the 1880s.[44] Cottage industry producers near Salonica were using about ten percent more wool in the 1890s than they had ca. 1800, a suggestion of ongoing vitality.[45] During the early twentieth century, some mechanized wool weaving factories emerged to supplement the hand-woven supplies but, unlike the home producers, required the finer grades of foreign wool.[46] The first significant mechanized cloth factory in the area, at Niaousta, became operational in 1908. In the next three years, two other mechanized wool weaving mills and a jute weaving factory, that made sacking for the booming tobacco industry, also opened in the city.[47]

Gürün, located roughly midway between Sivas and Malatya in Anatolia, was another important center of wool cloth production. It had prospered during the early part of the century, thanks to nomadic Kurds and Turkmen who pastured nearby. Local agriculture was poor and the townspeople had come to rely on the tribal migrations, supplying the tribes with their needs, including the textiles of Damascus, Aleppo, and Rize, and taking payment in wool. The merchants exported some of the wool directly but also distributed it nearby for spinning and weaving. By the 1830s, in addition, Gürün artisans annually were importing several thousand pieces of British calico, dyeing it blue and re-exporting the entire lot.[48] A half century later, Gürün's textile producers were working on 500 looms to weave shawls, trousers, and jackets from wool, as well as some light silk fabrics. They used homespun wool from local sources but mostly British yarn, preferred for its strength.[49] At this time, Gürün weavers specialized in light weaves, an imitation cashmere worn in summer, and made other cloth copied after Indian, Persian, and European patterns. Well-made and inexpensive, these were in strong demand locally and outside the province.[50] Gürün makers expanded their market in the early twentieth century, selling to Diyarbakır consumers for the first time in 1907 and initiating sales in the Egyptian market three years later.[51] They perhaps also had shifted from weaving only pure wool textiles to also making a fabric of cotton mixed with wool. The looms in 1911 numbered 3,500 and annual cloth production was triple the total just ten years before. Gürün had become the leading textile center in Sivas province.[52]

Cotton cloth making was commonplace in almost every region of the Ottoman Middle East, made by thousands of part- and full-time weavers working for personal needs and for the market. Commercial activities focused solely on working with cotton cloth were centered in several locations, notably in the Anatolian provinces. Tokat, in northern Anatolia, long had been famed for its cotton prints. These town artisans maintained their reputation and markets by shifting over to British cloth, during the 1830s at the latest. The town relied on good quality water and cheap labor for its reputation. By the early twentieth century, it also benefited from the presence of family members who lived in Manchester and shipped cloth home, thus avoiding the more costly intervention of outsiders.[53] Tokat specialized in making a headware of light cotton material (*yemeni*). Large pieces of the cloth first were printed with black patterns and dyed with the desired basic color. Patterns then were hand stamped in three to six colors. The dyehouses and workshops typically were small in scale: 150 dyeing and printing enterprises in the town ca. 1900 employed 1,800 workers. In addition, some 600 looms wove *manusa* cloth, using mainly British yarn that they dyed on the spot. The industry supplied buyers throughout Anatolia.[54]

Commercial cotton cloth manufacturing at Arapkir, northwest of Harput, owed its very existence to British yarn that the townspeople adopted in ca. 1830, beginning an industry that lasted throughout the century. Because the cloth was cheaper and more durable, British cloth (*nankeens*) quickly disappeared from the market. The number of looms jumped to 1,000 in 1836 and remained stable until the 1880s, when it increased perhaps twenty percent.[55]

In the very late nineteenth century, Aintab textile makers carved a market niche, producing a particular kind of cotton cloth, revealing the refined division of labor that existed among regional manufacturers. Between the 1870s and 1900, the number of looms at Aintab, a city some 100 km north of Aleppo, doubled, mainly weaving an inexpensive red cotton cloth that formerly had been made in Aleppo. Aleppo producers attempted to keep their customers by using imported synthetic dyes, both high-quality alizarin and the cheaper but photo-sensitive aniline dyes, and imported white yarn, thus dropping their costs a full ten percent.[56] But the gamble failed as even the alizarin red faded and created disgruntled customers. And so, after 1899, Aleppo weavers abandoned the experiment and resumed their imports of imported red yarn.[57] But, Aintab weavers adopted precisely the opposite tactic and, from 1904, used only yarn dyed in the city, reducing the costs of colored yarn by some fifty percent.[58] The colors were not as fast as the yarn dyed in Europe but were cheaper and met the peasant buyers' demands. Thus, Aintab cornered one part of the lower end of the market once held by Aleppo and, in the early twentieth century, specialized in making red cloth.[59]

While producers in locations such as Arapkir and Aintab specialized in certain cotton cloths, commercial weavers in other centers were more diversified, making many different kinds of cloth. The town of Diyarbakır and surrounding villages and the areas around Erzurum and Harput in eastern Anatolia, ca. 1870, held an estimated 11,700 looms. Two-thirds worked in the countryside weaving cotton cloth and the balance were town-based, making silk, mixed, and cotton cloths. Our first glimpse at the nineteenth-century industry in Diyarbakır reveals a dynamic and versatile sector, engaged in making a wide variety of cotton, silk, cotton-silk, and woolen textiles. Its international export market had vanished and the producers were focusing on meeting domestic Ottoman needs. The local market absorbed about one-fifth of the output and the balance was distributed along a network that reached north into Anatolia, south into Syria, and southeast into the Iraqi regions. Weavers had accepted British cotton yarn during the 1830s, and used it as well as homespun, that remained a vital part of the industry. The town of Diyarbakır during the 1850s contained just over 300 weaving establishments directed by 200 masters. Altogether, 1,500 men and boys worked on 1,200 looms.[60] Piece work prevailed, the rates varying by the type and size of textile being woven. Town weavers specialized in silk and cotton-silk textiles, including red and white-thread *kutni* and *çitari* as well as silk cloth (*canfez*) while most workers in the surrounding rural districts made cotton cloth.

The Diyarbakır region also enjoyed a "great manufacturing revival", that began in ca. 1870 and continued until World War I—one based on attention to the changing demands of customers in shifting economic conditions. In the highly competitive cotton cloth sector, for example, local producers carefully mixed cheap labor inputs and British materials: artisans used imported unbleached, red cotton, woolen yarns and plain cloth and wove or stamped the cloths with local, cheaper, labor. Between the 1860s and 1880s, local piece rates for cotton cloth seem to have fallen by a full fifty percent. Between the 1860s and 1908, cotton cloth production doubled while output of the famed cotton-silk cloth at least remained stable. Within the town of Diyarbakır itself, textile manufacturing perhaps reached record heights during the early twentieth century.[61]

Artisans in Aleppo similarly produced a vast variety of textiles. A major pillar of its international fame in earlier centuries had rested on indigo-dyed textiles, made from bleached cotton cloth woven in the city and surrounding villages. In earlier times, these blue textiles had formed nearly all of Aleppine cloth exports to France but, during the eighteenth century, French merchants at Aleppo shifted over to buying only bleached or raw cloth. Indigo dyeing for the export trade thus sharply declined in importance.[62]

The many details that are available concerning the Aleppo textile industry offer a fine case study of the sensitivity of Ottoman merchants and artisans to quickly changing conditions. Three examples will suffice to make the point. When competing silk weaving factories at Damascus were destroyed during the riots of 1860, for example, the number of active looms at Aleppo immediately rose fifty percent to 6,000, to supply the Egyptian market. Similarly, when the American Civil War pushed cotton prices through the roof and first affected the price of British textiles, Aleppo producers saw their temporary price advantage and seized the British T cloth market in Diyarbakır and Baghdad. By the end of 1861, as local raw cotton prices also rose enormously, they abandoned the effort. And, when the last killing famine of the nineteenth century struck Anatolia during the 1870s, sales collapsed and Aleppo weavers put away their looms. Many weavers migrated to other provinces and to Egypt for work but came back and resumed work when the crisis ended.[63]

In Ottoman historiographical literature, Aleppo has been cited as a major example of industrial decline. This decline, however, was in the eyes of the beholders and not in reality. Put simply, European consuls and other Western contemporaries carelessly presented statistics to demonstrate the decline they were convinced must have occurred. They established the decline of the Aleppo industry in their own day by comparing it with production levels of the past. To give just one example: a consul at Aleppo in 1862 proved the manufacturing collapse in the city by comparing the 3,650 looms of 1862 with the 10,000 looms that he said were present just a decade before. But a consular official in 1871 used the 1860s as the basis for comparison. He proved the sharp decline of the Aleppo industry by comparing the 5,000 looms then operating, in 1871, with the 10,000 looms that he said had been present ten years before.[64]

Rather than declining, nineteenth-century Aleppo textile producers were encountering constantly changing conditions, as we have seen. Wars, political instability, international crises, or crop failures affecting their peasant customers depressed output and caused many weavers to put away their looms, waiting for better times. A return to normal conditions, bumper crops, or the misfortunes of the city's competitors brought the weavers back to the looms. Thus, downward shifts in the number of looms operating do not show decline but they do reflect widely fluctuating market opportunities. In most years of the nineteenth century, between 3 to 6,000 looms actively wove; but the number often fell below 3,000 and sometimes to 1,500 and less. The number of artisans making gold and silver thread—important in the luxury silk textiles—actually increased slightly between 1838 and 1902. Also, the number of dyehouses in Aleppo remained steady and probably increased over the nineteenth century. In ca. 1838, there were perhaps 100 dyeshops (and printshops) while, in 1899, there were 129 operating, together with twenty-seven printing factories. In 1901, approximately 100 dyehouses worked in indigo alone while, by 1907, the number had reached 120, using both synthetic and natural indigo.[65] In addition, trends in the use of domestic and imported cotton yarn demonstrate a pattern of stability between the mid 1850s and early 1870s and then very sharp growth.[66] By 1905, cotton yarn usage was four to eight times greater than it had been in the 1850s to 1870s.[67] Thus, it seems clear that textile production hardly was declining.

Similarly, the trend in textile exports from Alexandretta/İskenderun support the argument for growth, at least during the period 1880–1911, for which data are available. These seaborne exports to İstanbul, İzmir, and the European provinces, ca. 1900, represented about one-half of total textile output in the area of North Syria. After remaining approximately steady from the early 1880s through ca. 1900, the value of textile exports then jumped more than fifty percent by 1908.[68] The port served as the outlet for the other textile centers of north Syria as well; these included Aintab, Maraş, Urfa and, to a lesser extent, Kilis. These export statistics thus point to the more general increase in textile production that was occurring in the North Syria region, where Aleppo was the first-ranked among a number of textile production centers.[69]

The great Ottoman capital city of İstanbul produced an extremely wide variety of textiles. It was not a major manufacturing center in the sense of supplying vast quantities of finished goods to the rest of the empire. The incredible size of its population, however, assured that İstanbul was the seat of important industrial activities keyed to furnishing local needs. Given the abiding concern of the state to tranquilize the residents of the imperial capital, the conditions of production probably are unique to the city. That is, the nature of İstanbul manufacturing likely is *sui generis.*

Its artisans had been among the first to feel the impact of European competition and changing government policy towards local manufacturers. Many İstanbul craft guilds were badly hurt when the state inaugurated the *Tanzimat* reforms, that assaulted long-standing monopolies in favor of freedom in the marketplace and in manufacturing. The state, thus, theoretically had abandoned its centuries-old effort to control industrial production. But in practice, the state played a mixed role, taking with the one hand, giving with the other. It upheld monopolies on behalf of some guilds, on other occasions it struck down guild privileges. Although these corporate groups must have been badly hurt when they lost monopolies, many textile guilds survived until the end of the century, at least in the official enumerations that were made.[70]

If the İstanbul guilds suffered and often died, many manufacturing activities continued and even expanded. İstanbul participated in the general revival of Ottoman manufacturing that took place in the final quarter of the nineteenth century. As elsewhere, the willingness of the local workers to accept very low wages played an important role. With its huge labor pool, excellent transportation and communication linkages, and large merchant community, conditions in the capital were particularly amenable to the growth of the low wage industries that prevailed in the later part of the century. Putting-out networks, for example, to make lace and to handpaint cotton veils and headcloths, employed many İstanbul women and girls working at home, both full- and part-time. The merchants in the one case exported the "Irish" lace to Western Europe and in the other sent the veils to Anatolia and Persia.[71] A similar development in lacemaking simultaneously occurred in the Aintab area, where local women used Belfast materials, under the direction of American missionaries.[72] By 1911, the agent of an Irish firm employed several hundred Aintab-area girls and women to make linen handkerchiefs and lacework, mostly for export to the United States.[73]

The rising availability of the sewing machine played an important role in several İstanbul sweatshop industries, including the manufacture of umbrellas and ready-made clothing and shoes. Sewing machines appeared in significant numbers on the Ottoman scene at the end of the century, when the Singer Company introduced cheap machines and installment buying. In the early twentieth century, thousands of the machines annually were being imported.[74]

At the end of the nineteenth century, as İstanbul became a major assemblage center of imported umbrella components from Europe, the trade in imported umbrellas came nearly to a complete halt. In common with the İstanbul lacemakers and veil painters, the low wages of umbrella assemblers—men, as well as large numbers of children and women— made them competitive. The assembled umbrellas were shipped to buyers in İstanbul, Salonica, Anatolia, İzmir and Beirut, as well as Bulgaria and Cairo. In ca. 1902, a local workshop began manufacturing umbrella handles, reducing the dependence on foreign materials.[75]

Similarly, a ready-made garment industry, directed by local department stores, thrived on the combination of imported materials and cheap labor. By 1900, sales of local ready-made clothing surpassed those of the imported product. The industry produced for both the top and the bottom of the market, in the latter case, employing labor of "incredible cheapness." Tailors employed their wives and children and several young workers and sewed for piece work wages. The final products sold for one-half or less the price of imports.[76]

PRODUCTION FOR THE INTERNATIONAL EXPORT MARKET

Silk

Silk production—raw silk reeling and cloth weaving—was an important economic activity throughout the nineteenth century. At its end, the industry in all its forms and in the various locations employed quite large numbers of people, more than 400,000 Ottoman subjects full- or part-time. In the Bursa region, some 150,000 persons worked full- and part-time and approximately the same number were employed in the Lebanon area. In addition, there were the silk weavers of Aleppo and Diyarbakır as well as the spinners of Edirne, Salonica, and other areas.

In this study, we will pass over the fascinating account of silk cloth production, that lost its international consumers but found new domestic ones as the century progressed.[77] Here, we focus on raw silk reeling, for the example that it provides of Ottoman manufacturers competing in the international export markets of the nineteenth century. Two secular trends coincided to prompt the rise of an export industry in raw silk. Abroad, European demand for raw silk sharply mounted as Western prosperity and per capita silk cloth consumption increased. On the domestic scene, Ottoman labor became available for increased raw silk production. Stagnating demand for Ottoman silk cloth during the 1820s and 1830s made some weavers redundant and available for other employment. Simultaneously, cheap imported cotton yarn freed erstwhile cotton spinners to take on silk spinning tasks that initially were more remunerative. Foreign and Ottoman merchants brought the new technologies and the necessary capital and were the catalyst that fused European demand for raw silk materials with newly available Ottoman labor supplies. They closely regulated hand-spinning output, seeking raw silk of more regular and higher qualities and, to this end, also introduced the so-called short reel. Until the later 1850s, these usually were placed in homes and small workshops. And finally, they established centralized factories and installed equipment, including short reels, sometimes driven by water but increasingly by steam power.

The short reels at Bursa first appeared in 1838 and, by 1860, accounted for ninety-eight percent of all raw silk reeled in the region.[78] Centralized reeling factories also appeared at Bursa in 1838, founded by a French family. Sustained by rising Western demand, the industry continued to expand and, by 1855, the Bursa region contained some 2,000 factory-based reels. They initially reeled a relatively uniform derneir but, by 1867, were producing different thicknesses to meet the varying European demands.[79]

Developments parallel to those in the Bursa reeling industry—the adoption of short reels and steam-powered mills to supply European buyers—simultaneously took place in many other Ottoman locations including, Salonica, the Lebanon, Amasya, and İzmir. Unusually, Diyarbakır reelers remained focused on the supply of Ottoman weavers, primarily those at Aleppo as well as in Diyarbakır itself.[80]

Already-impressive achievements in factory-based, short reel steam reeling were surpassed because of silkworm disease epidemics in Europe. Appearing in France and Italy by 1853, the diseases destroyed the silkworms and wrecked havoc with European raw silk production. The burgeoning silk industries there desperately needed raw silk as well as uninfected eggs and cocoons and were willing to pay exceptionally high prices. Disease in Europe, the rapid rise of factory-based silk reeling and correspondingly inflated local cocoon prices combined to accelerate the abandonment of Bursa hand reeling in favor of cocoon raising and factory employ by many villagers.[81] The families' abandonment of hand reeling gained additional momentum in the decade after 1845 and the number of reeling mills climbed steadily, to twenty-nine in 1855. Then, as Ottoman and foreign merchants frantically sought to fill the disease-created gap in Europe's supply, the number of mills leapfrogged, rising to eighty-three in 1860.

But silkworm diseases began attacking the Ottoman silk industry and many mill operators went bankrupt or suspended operations.[82] For decades, entrepreneurs at Bursa unsuccessfully tried a number of remedies for the disease, including the import of disease-free silkworm eggs. A method to end the crisis appeared after 1870, thanks to five years of research by Louis Pasteur. The great French scientist found a relatively simple technique to control and essentially eliminate these silkworm diseases, one involving microscopes to identify healthy eggs and cocoons and so rebuild a sound population. Widespread adoption of these remedies, however, was slow because of continuous declines in international silk prices, caused by the massive entry of East Asian silk into Europe. After 1869, the newly opened Suez Canal promoted the flow of huge quantities of raw silk from China and Japan. During the early 1870s, Oriental raw silk exports already were seven times greater than those from the entire Middle East. Global raw silk prices fell steadily until 1892 and then bottomed out, at levels sharply lower than those prevailing in 1868.

In the post-1892 era of price stability, many new mills were opened, especially at Bursa but also in Edirne and the Lebanon.[83] The number of mills in the Bursa region rose by fifty percent as regional annual raw silk production rose fourfold, from about 154 tons in the early 1890s to about 677 tons, during the next two decades. Overall, during this same period, aggregate Middle East raw silk production (the statistics here include Russia and the Balkan states) rose from 1,100 to 2,800 tons.

Thus, production boomed. But prices did not. After 1892, international nominal raw silk prices evidenced a slight upward tendency but each time prices climbed somewhat, there was a very sharp fall, followed by a gradual rise and another price collapse. In 1910, the price of raw silk was only about ten percent higher than it had been in 1892. Moreover, this very modest rise occurred in the context of a substantial increase in general commodity prices that took place after the end of the world depression in 1896. Overall, the price trend for raw silk through 1914 was unfavorable for producers.

Throughout the century, both the factory workers and the mill operators suffered from the nature of the silk industry. Workers were particularly hurt by the wage-price trends in the later part of the period but were poorly paid during almost the entire long nineteenth century. Nominal wages at Bursa more or less had doubled between the first decade of factory reeling and the proliferation of silk mills in the later 1850s, as employers recruited a workforce for the new industry. But, by the end of the 1860s wages had fallen to levels that were twenty to forty percent below their 1857 peak.[84] Thereafter, wage data are available only at the very end of the period, in 1913. At that time, reelers' wages at Bursa were the lowest among all Ottoman factory workers.[85] In real wage terms, moreover, there clearly had been a significant decline after the 1860s.

Silk mill operators, for their part, competed in a business that during a brief period each year required relatively vast amounts of capital to buy the cocoons for reeling. Chronically short of cash, the operators frantically sought to be the first to ship bales of silk to Europe. With the gold or credit obtained, often from Lyon and Milan, they continued to buy cocoons and thus keep their mills running for the rest of the season. Over capacity or, to put it another way, inadequate supplies of cocoons, plagued the industry throughout the century, both in times of healthy and diseased silkworms, in periods of boom as well as of bust. During the crisis of the later 1860s, the factories at Bursa had the annual capacity to reel 700,000 lbs. of silk but had supplies for only 393,000 lbs. Thirty years later, disease was under control and production was booming. Capacity had expanded vastly by the early twentieth century but still was double the amount of raw silk being reeled from the available supplies of cocoons.[86] But, because of East Asian production, price trends for raw silk were not favorable and there was very severe pressure to minimize costs. Thus, even under the strong market conditions that prevailed at the end of the century, considerable uncertainty remained in the industry. The combination of fierce competition for cocoons and capital scarcity meant that many mills operated part time. Some factories reportedly stood idle for up to six and seven months per year, profiting neither entrepreneur nor worker.[87] Ottoman silk reeling remained an industry of exceptional volatility, a risky investment for capitalists and a low-paying, irregular, and undependable job for workers.

Carpet Making

The making of so-called oriental rugs is easily the most well-known industrial activity of the late Ottoman period.[88] This is not because of the workers' behavior or characteristics or even the important place of rug making in the late Ottoman economy but rather derives from the special place of carpets in the Western aesthetic tradition that imagines each rug as a uniquely fashioned art object. The reality, however, is quite different. In fact, these rugs were (and are) mass-produced goods turned out by thousands of workers—oftentimes children—in sweatshop conditions.

Rug making in Anatolia, the center of the industry, is often associated with the arrival of the nomadic Turkish tribes who settled down around the town of Uşak. The relationship between Ottoman carpet producer and Western consumer reaches back to at least the sixteenth century, when rugs began to be sent abroad and found their way into the paintings of Holbein and others. At that time, caravans of horses, camels, and wagons full of rugs already were finding their way to Europe. Purchased mainly by the upper classes, these were medium to coarse-grade rugs, produced in comparatively large quantities for export. The foreign market developed further during the early eighteenth century and by its end, a sizeable and well-organized export industry in carpets existed in western Anatolia.[89] Commercial rug making continued to grow during the first half of the nineteenth century.

A decisive shift occurred, that may have taken place as early as 1825, when carpet buying became common among broader segments of European and American society.[90] The maturing of industrialization in the West brought comparatively greater incomes and a rising consumerism and Europeans and Americans adopted increasingly lavish tastes in furniture and home decoration. Rugs played an important role and, as the nineteenth century wore on, Oriental carpets nearly reached the level of a mass consumption item, becoming a familiar part of Western everyday life.

Beginning not later than the 1850s, Ottoman rug making witnessed a growth that authentically can be called extraordinary. Rug exports from İzmir, that remained the major exit point for the rugs, doubled in the two decades after 1857, doubled again by the late 1890s and, incredibly, doubled yet again in the period before World War I.

These sharp rises in rug production derived from the combination of Western taste changes with the Ottomans' need for remittances to pay for the soaring imports of European goods that followed the Napoleonic wars.[91] Cash-short peasants and merchants seeking to buy imports found the means to do business in the commercial production of carpets. The need for carpets to finance imports certainly heightened during the collapse of Ottoman raw silk production between the 1860s and the early 1880s, when the cash income from silk suddenly vanished. There probably is some relationship between the fates of Ottoman silk reeling and carpet making during the third quarter of the nineteenth century.

The particular appeal of the rugs to Westerners as unique, handmade goods, shaped the industry in a singular way. Nearly everything concerning rugs changed to make them more saleable and their production faster and more efficient. New designs were introduced to meet Western tastes while the wool yarn finally became machine-made to relieve labor shortages, although many merchants remained unhappy with the shift. Artificial and synthetic dyestuffs were adopted, rejected, and re-adopted while merchants sought to centralize the dyeing process itself. Knotting the rugs increasingly moved from households to workshops. But through all these changes there was one constant—the loom. Thus, the rug was still handmade.

Several west Anatolian towns, notably Uşak but also Gördes and Kula, long had dominated the industry; in the 1870s, Uşak accounted for some three-quarters of total rug output in Anatolia. During the post-1850 boom, commercial rug making increased sharply in these towns and also expanded into hundreds of other towns and villages. Some 2,000 looms, for example, were placed into commercial production at Sivas during the late nineteenth century. Similarly, at İsparta, 800 looms went into production not sooner than ca. 1900. There were at least 8,000 looms in commercial operation in Anatolia ca. 1906 as compared to perhaps 2,000 in the early 1880s.[92]

Government officials sometimes took the initiative and introduced the new craft but the major agents of the diffusion were merchant houses, primarily those at İzmir and secondarily at İstanbul. Merchants independent of these houses—notably at Uşak—played an important role as well. Most of the merchant firms seem to have been foreign but some, such as one that entered the Uşak rug trade in 1772, were Ottoman.

By the beginning of the twentieth century, some ninety percent of the İzmir rug trade had concentrated in six merchant houses of European origin. Three had been operating in İzmir since about the late 1830s. An American firm had been in the İzmir carpet trade since the 1830s.[93] The İstanbul houses, by contrast, largely had not been involved in Anatolian rugmaking, focusing instead on the trade in carpets from Persia. Towards the end of the century, however, some İstanbul merchants entered the Anatolian industry, with important consequences (discussed later).

Missionaries also set up rugmaking operations quite late in the period. At Urfa, a German charitable organization formed a carpet 'factory' while, at Harput, American capital was responsible, directed by an

Ottoman subject who had trained in U.S. carpet factories. A similar rug workshop, employing 600 to 700 girls and women, seems to have operated at Aleppo.[94]

The emergence of nineteenth-century carpet making in the Sivas region typifies the expansion of the industry. Until ca. 1890, rugs were being made only in the countryside around the town of Sivas. Then the governor introduced Khurasanian and Persian designs and established some 300 looms, scattered about in the town itself. The rugs produced were different in color and design and were much finer than the country rugs.[95] Following this, three Ottoman Armenians in 1900 formed a company to mass produce rugs in the town. They set up a twenty loom workshop with eighty workers, managed by a young Armenian who had gone to America and worked in the carpet business there.[96] An agent of an İzmir merchant house then arrived, offering advances and a guaranteed market but lower wages.[97] Just two years later, there were as many as 2,000 looms working in the city. Several grand workshops emerged, each holding hundreds of looms, with nearly 1,000 female workers, making rugs that rivalled the better Persian grades. In 1911, the rug factories in Sivas employed "many thousand little [Armenian] girls," in addition to a large number of home looms.[98] Altogether, the district reportedly contained some 10,000 rug looms.[99]

In the city of Konya, several İstanbul merchant houses and the Ottoman governor worked to develop the export rug industry. The local governor held a forty-day rug exhibition, displaying old carpets next to modern Anatolian ones, in order to stimulate the industry and give knotters some models for their craft. The British vice-consul, on behalf of an İstanbul rug firm, developed an extensive network that made good quality rugs totalling, in 1900, 20,000 meters.[100] In the province of Konya İstanbul houses then controlled some 2,350 looms.

The threat to the hegemony of the İzmir houses was clear. Moreover, the activities of İstanbul merchant houses in Konya were not unique but part of their larger and successful effort to enter Anatolian rug making. Still worse, the İstanbul merchants' actions were accompanied by a more widespread attack on the position of the İzmir houses. For example, three consortia of Uşak Muslim rug merchants founded as many wool spinning mills around the turn of the century.

The timing was critical; the international market was huge and booming and the demand for the rugs apparently was insatiable. Who would control and benefit from the boom? Hence, the emergence of the İzmir-based Oriental Carpet Manufacturers Ltd. (OCM), founded in 1908.

The trust included most İzmir merchants who established it to protect their position and maintain control over the expanding market. In the end, the OCM İzmir merchants were the major victors, essentially driving their İstanbul rivals from the market. By 1912, for example, the province of Konya held some 4,000 looms with 15 to 20,000 working girls, more than three times the number in 1906. The great majority worked for the Oriental Carpet Manufacturers as the İstanbul presence had vanished.[101] In Anatolia generally, the OCM controlled most of the looms working for the market. Some of the Uşak merchant/manufacturers, however, survived the OCM onslaught and remained prominent in the industry.

Throughout the period, almost all carpet knotters were girls and women although men commonly were the professional dyers and, occasionally, the knotters. Also, the division of labor became more pronounced as commercial production advanced over the century. Thus, it became increasingly unusual to find a single person or family spinning, dyeing, and knotting. Reflecting this more refined division of labor, the household relatively diminished in importance as the site of the various phases of carpet making. Workshop production became more important in the final knotting stage while factory production increasingly replaced both workshop and household labor in the spinning and dyeing phases of production. Workers and merchants prospered most during the early part of the period but then respectively encountered stable or falling wages and rug prices. Overall, between the 1830s and 1880s, prices for some grades of Uşak rugs increased three- and fivefold while knotters' nominal wages doubled. Thereafter, the picture was less rosy. Between 1882 and ca. 1900, carpet prices may have climbed slightly and then remained steady during the first decade of the century, thus stagnating during the post-1896 period of general price inflation. Knotters' nominal wages at Uşak remained unchanged after 1882 while, in the areas of new production wages also were stable but lower. Their real wages fell during the general price rise after 1896 and perhaps as early as the 1880s. Similar to their sisters in silk reeling, carpet knotters were mired in a low-wage industry with declining real wages at the end of the period.[102]

NOTES

1. Here, I am rejecting the calculations of Pamuk (1987), who attempted to estimate total Ottoman consumption of textiles. He does give us a good summary of cloth and yarn imports but, as I have shown elsewhere, he grossly understates the volume of Ottoman yarn production. (See Quataert, 1993b).

2. United States National Archives (USNA), Film T194, Constantinople Dispatches, Reel 3,—/18/1858; Consular Reports of the United States (CRUS) for year ending 9/30/1859; France, Bulletin Consulaire Français. *Recueil des rapports commerciaux...par agents diplomatiques et consulaires de France à l'étranger* (BCF) 1879, Smyrne, 2 Avril 1879.

3. France, *Rapports commerciaux des agents diplomatiques et consulaires de France* (RCC), microfilms of BCF, Reel 35, Izmir for 1902; from Germany, Handel und Industrie, *Berichte über Handel und Industrie* (Buhi) 1913, 9/24/1912, 18; Stich (1929), 88.

4. *La Revue Commerciale du Levant* (RCL) 31 Mai 1904 is a special issue on yarns that has considerable information on the comparative importance of imported and domestic, as well as dyed and undyed, yarns. Compare Scherzer (1873) with Great Britain (GB) *Annual Series* (AS) 5247, Smyrna for 1912–1913.

5. Buhi, III, Heft 10, 1/22/1902 Aleppo; Buhi x, Heft 9; Buhi, Heft 13, 2/14/1902. Austria, *Berichte der k. und k. Österr.-Ung. Konsularämter über das Jahr* (k und k), 1907, VIII, 1, Aleppo.

6. Buhi, X, Heft 9, 8/20/1907; RCL 31 Mai 1904, Lettre de Marache; Buhi Heft 13, 2/14/1902.

7. RCC Reel 34, Nr.150, Trebizonde for 1901. Buhi, IV, 13, 11/20/1902.

8. GB Accounts and Papers (A&P) 1896, 89, Richards, Ankara for 1895, 5/8/1896.

9. RCC Reel 32, #271, Commerce of İzmir for 1893; this probably was used in rug manufacturing.

10. See Issawi (1982), 150–161, for a good summary of the arguments.

11. For example, Georgiades (1873), 73–74.

12. İstanbul, Başbakanlık Arşivi (BBA) Meclis-i Mahsus (MM) 2474, İradeler, 17 Ş 1294 and *Düstur*, birinci tertip, IV (İstanbul, 1289–1302), 427–428; Buhi 1904; BBA Bab-ı Âli Evrak Odası (BEO) 100210, 27 Safer 1318/1900.

13. See, for example, Clark (1969).

14. Issawi (1982), 156.

15. See, for example, Buhi I 16, 5/26/1900.

16. My thanks to Albert Feuerwerker, University of Michigan, Ann Arbor, for his comparisons of the Ottoman Empire and Qing China.

17. BBA MM 2274, 12 r 1292/1875.

18. (GB) Foreign Office (FO) 195/687, 4/20/1861.

19. GB AS 4579, Salonica for 1909.

20. GB AS 4538,Trebizond for 1909.

21. Quataert, (1986), 473–489.

22. Buhi, X, Heft 9, 8/20/1907.

23. GB AS 5247, Smyrna for 1912–1913; RCL 31 Mai 1904. GB AS 2950, Constantinople for 1902; GB AS 3140, Constantinople for 1903. GB AS 3170, Smyrna for 1901–1903; Buhi, Januar 1902, III, Heft 9; RCL 31 Mai 1904.

24. Luckerts (1906), 19–34. A&P 1896, 89, Richards at Ankara for 1895, 5/18/1896.

25. Pamuk (1987), using the 1911 borders of the empire as the unit of comparison.

26. İnalcık (1979–1980), 1–65. BBA Cev Harc 2133 Ca 1207 and 2677 Ca 1207/1793; Cev İkt 1114, 25 S 1228/1813.

27. BBA Cev Mal 652, 4 S 1245/1829.

28. BBA Hatt-i Hümayun (HH) 51599, 51599a–b, 1250/1834-5; Meclis-i Vala (MV) 13393, 3 Ş 1271/1855; Cev İkt 1415 1229/1814.

29. İnalcık (1979–80); Cunningham (1983), 77. Pamuk (1987).

30. Pamuk (1987).

31. For example, see the works by Issawi for a presentation of the geography argument.

32. USNA T 238, reel 2, 12/31/1843, D. Offley; at this time, the city shipped $10 million in raw cotton.

33. GB FO 78/289, 11 November 1836 and 11 May 1836, Brant at Trebizond.

34. Nuri (1922).

35. USNA T681, Jewett at Sivas, 5/26/1887 and 5/26/1893.

36. RCC, Reel 34, Nr. 149, Sivas in 1901; Buhi, X, Heft 9, 8/10/1907.

37. GB A&P 1859, 30, Skene on 1857 Aleppo trade; Buhi, I, Heft 9, 8/20/1907.

38. Buhi, X, Heft 9, 8/20/1907, noting the use of 10,000 packets of regional yarn. Usual packet weight was 4.5 kgs; 1.28 kgs per *okke*. In addition, the weavers purchased yarn from the Adana mills.

39. Buhi, X, Heft 9, 8/20/1907. The total cotton harvest equalled 2.1 million pounds. RCL 5/31/1904, Lettre de Harpout, 1 Avril 1904. Cotton yarn "chiefly is made by villagers who avail themselves of their distaffs in traversing the wheel."

40. See for example, GB FO 195/113, Sandison at Bursa, 2/15/1840; FO 195/208. Sandison at Bursa, 3/10/1844, report on Bursa trade for 1843; FO 78/750, report on Bursa trade for 1847. FO 195/393, Sandison at Bursa, 1/28/1861 shows the prolonged duration of the fashion changes.

41. Pamuk (1987), 115.

42. See Owen, (1981) and the various works by Issawi for this position.

43. *Selanik Vilayeti Salnamesi* (*VS*) 1307/1889, 228.

44. *Selanik VS* 1307/1889, 227.

45. GB AS 1886, 24, Salonica for 1883–4 and AS 1887, 75, Salonica for 1885; GB AS 1888, 394, Salonica for 1887; AS 1889, 623, Salonica for 1888; A&P 1896, 89, Blunt, Salonica for 1893–4; k und k, 1906, XXI, 3 Salonich.

46. k und k 1906, XXI, 3, Salonich.

47. Buhi, XIX, Heft 6, April 13, 1913, 444–446.

48. GB FO 78/289, Brant, 8/11/1836 and 3/11/1836.

49. Cuinet (1890), I , 650, 693; Buhi, 1904, gives the number as 400, in Christian hands.

50. *Sivas VS 1306*/1888, 217; Sivas VS 1321/1903, 181; k und k 1903, Konstantinopel.

51. GB A&P 1908, 117, 7253, Shipley, Erzeroom for 1907; RCC Anneé 1911, Sivas Vilayet, #953, Reel 40.

52. RCC Anneé 1911, Sivas Vilayet, #953, Reel 40.

53. GB FO 78/289, 3/31/1836 and 11/11/1836. Buhi, IV, 13, 11/20/1902, Trapezunt.

54. Buhi, 9, 8/20/1907. GB A&P 1898, 94, 6125, Ankara, Shipley, 7/11/1898; A&P 1913, 73, 7781, Monahan for 1912.

55. GB FO 78/289, 11 May 1836 and 8 November 1836, Brant at Trebizond, who says that the Armenians were chiefly engaged in this production. USNA T681, H.M. Jewett, 3/1/1888. GB AS 1886, Erzeroum for 1885.

56. GB A&P 1893–94, 97, 5581,Jago, Aleppo, 7 April 1893.

57. Buhi III, 10, 22 Januar 1902, Aleppo. Buhi, x, Heft 9, 8/20/1907.

58. Dyeing ten pounds of British yarn in Europe then cost c. 5 kronen while dyeing it 'Turkish red' in Aintab cost only 2.5 kronen. k und k, 1904, I, 1. In 1902, Aintab had imported 600,000 kgs of better quality red yarn. Buhi Heft 13, 2/14/1902.

59. e.g., k und k 1907, VIII, 1, Aleppo; Buhi, 9, 20 August 1907, Aleppo.

60. GB FO 78/289, Brant at Trebizond, November 8, 1836; FO 195/459, Holmes on Pashalık of Diarbekir, April 14, 1857 and Holmes at Diarbekir, March 31, 1857; A&P 1865, 53, Taylor for 1863; FO 195/799, Taylor at Diarbekir, January 11, 1864 and March 31, 1864.

61. A&P 1873, 67, Taylor, 14 November 1872. Compare the piece rates for *şeytan bezi* in FO 195/799, Trade and Agriculture of Kurdistan for 1863, Taylor at İstanbul, July 1864 with 1888 piece rate for cotton cloth production in the town of Diyarbakır in BCF 1880, Diarbakır 1 Juli 1889. (See also Quataert (1993b) for additional details.)

62. Fukasawa (1987), 51–53.

63. GB FO 195/700, Skene at Aleppo, 31 December 1860 and 8 June 1861. GB A&P 1877, 83, 4024, Skene for 1876; FO AS 1889, 500, Jago at Aleppo, 6 March 1889.

64. Ibid. and additional GB A&P reports from Aleppo.

65. GB FO 195/902, Skene, Aleppo, 2 April 1868; *Halep VS* 1317/1899, 191–2; k und k X, 3, 1901, Aleppo; k und k VIII,1, 1907, Aleppo.

66. CRUS Aleppo for Year Ending 30 September 1858, Aleppo for 1857, 348; GB A&P 1872, LVII, 3565, Skene at Aleppo, 31 December 1871.

67. Buhi, Heft 13, 14 February 1902; see Issawi (1988), 144.

68. See Quataert (1993b), for the statistics, drawn from British consular sources.

69. Ibid. and Fukasawa (1987), 47, 51–52.

70. BBA İradeler, MM 4031, 12 cr 1304/March 1887.

71. Dumont (1982), 220. BCF 1889, Trebizonde.

72. GB A&P 1905, 93, 6884, Aleppo, 31 March 1905.

73. GB A&P 1912–13, 100, 7685, Fontana at Aleppo; A&P 1914, 95, 7883, Fontana at Aleppo. To capture some of this thriving business, a number of local entrepreneurs established their own networks, manufacturing the hankies and lacework for direct export to America.

74. For details, see Quataert (1992).

75. Buhi 1904, 322–323; Herlt (1918), 41–80.

76. RCL, 31 Octobre 1909, 440–446; Herlt (1918). Buhi 14 Februar 1902, Heft 13, 522–523, shows similar patterns of very cheap labor producing ready-made clothing in İzmir and Beirut.

77. For details of silk cloth production, see Quataert (1993b).

78. GB FO 195/393, 20 March 1854, Sandison at Bursa; A&P 1862, 58, Sandison at Bursa for 1860. GB FO 195/774, Sandison for 1864, 16 August 1865. In 1901, 103 hand reels still worked in the city of Bursa, four percent of all reels operating. RCC Turquie, Brousse, 25 Mars 1898.

79. Stich (1929), 96. Cuinet (1894) IV, 57–8; USNA Film T 19, Reel 2, 1 October 1847, Schwaabe; GB FO 195/205, Sandison at Bursa, 25 June 1845. Dalsar (1960), 410–412. The French migration and establishment of the French silk producers' colony at Bursa certainly is tied to the great strikes in the silk center of Lyons between 1831–1834 and in subsequent years. Sewell (1980) 207–208, 217. Delbeuf (1906), 131.

80. GB FO 195/100, 31 December 1838 and FO 195/176, 2 February 1843 and FO 195/240, 27 March 1846, Blunt at Salonica; FO 78/441 and CR US 1851, T 194, Reel 3. GB FO, *Factories* (1873). Compare with RCC 1905, #412 and RCC 1910, Adrianople province for 1903 and 1909.

81. GB A&P 1854–55, LV, 2264, Sandison at Bursa for 1854. RCL 31 Julliet 1901, 154–155.

82. GB FO *Factories* (1873), J. Maling at Brussa, 5 October 1872. Similar patterns of boom then collapse and the closing of factories occurred in the other production centers.

83. GB FO *Factories* (1873); RCC 1910, Adrianople for 1909, 8–9. RCC 1910, #838, Adrianople for 1908.

84. GB FO 78/905, 8 August 1852 and other Sandison reports from Bursa; GB FO *Factories* (1973); Turkey (1970), 21–23.

85. *Turkey* (1970) 1917 table VIII, 23 and Table VIII, 21. J. Maling at Bursa, October 5, 1872 in GB FO *Factories* (1873).

86. J. Maling October 5, 1872 report in GB FO *Factories* (1873) and RCL 31 August 1901, 353–4; k und k 1901, X, 4, Brussa, says that the industry required 8.5 million kgs. of cocoon but had only 4.5 million kgs.

87. RCL 31 Janvier 1901, 488–490, 493 and 31 Julliet 1901, 154–155.

88. Except when directly cited, I will not refer to the vast literature on carpets/rugs as art objects. See Quataert (1986) for more details and sources.

89. *Turkey* (1968), 254–260; BBA HH 56146, 1204/1789–90.

90. *Turkey* (1968), 267.

91. For examples from the Uşak region, see GB FO 195/288, statement of the sums due to Messers. Werry, Keun and Company, 1846.

92. See Quataert (1993b) for details and sources.

93. Stich (1929), 23–24; and personal interview with Howard Reed, August 1983, about his American ancestor, Blackler.

94. US Department of Commerce and Labor, Bureau of Manufacturing, *Turkey for 1907.* CRUS LXIX, 262, July 1902; Harput, 7 April 1902, Norton. GB AS 4741, Aleppo for 1910, 5.

95. RCL Lettre de Sivas 8 Août 1900.

96. GB A&P 1901, 85, 6450, Trebizond; also RCL Lettre de Sivas, 8 Août 1900, 207; repeated in Buhi 1906, 9, 727.

97. RCC reel #34, Nr 149, Sivas in 1901, 14, Grenard, vice-consul for France. *Sivas VS* 1321/1903, 180.

98. Buhi 9, 1906, 727.

99. *Sivas VS* 1321/1903, 180; Luckerts (1906); Buhi 1906, 9, 727.

100. RCL 1900, Lettre de Koniah, 28 Août 1900, 238–9. RCC 1907, #613, Smyrne for 1905.

101. *Levant Trade Review* June 1912, 92. Quataert (1993b).

102. See Quataert (1993b) for additional details and sources.

REFERENCES CITED

Austria, *Berichte der k. und k. Öster.-Ung. Konsularämter über das Jahr...*

Başbakanlık Arşivi (İstanbul), Bab-ı Âli Evrak Odası.
    Cevdet: Hariciye; İktisat; Maliye.
    Hatt-i Hümayun.
    İradeler.
    Meclis-i Mahsus.
    Meclis-i Vala.

Clark, Edward C.
    1969   "The Emergence of Textile Manufacturing Entrepreneurs in Turkey," Ph.D. Dissertation, Princeton University.

Cunningham, A.B.
    1983   "The Journal of Christophe Aubin: A Report on the Levant Trade in 1812," *Archivum Ottomanicum*, 8.

Cuinet, Vital
  1890–
    1894   L*a Turquie d'Asie; Géographie Administrative Statistique Descriptive et Raisonnée de Chaque Province De l'Asie Mineure.* 4 vols.

Dalsar, Fahri
  1960   *Bursa'da İpekçilik.* İstanbul.

Delbeuf, Régis
  1906   *Une Excursion à Brousse et à Nicée.* Constantinople.

Dumont, Paul
  1982   "Jewish Communities in Turkey During the Last Decades of the XIXth Century in the Light of the Archives of the Alliance Israelite Universelle," in Benjamin Braude and Bernard Lewis, eds., *Christians and Jews in the Ottoman Empire*, I, New York.

France   *Rapports commerciaux des agents diplomatiques et consulaires de France.*

Fukasawa, Katsumi
  1987   *Toilerie et Commerce du Levant d'Alep à Marseille.* Paris.

Georgiades, D.
  1873   *Smyrne et l'Asie Mineure.* Paris.

Germany   *Berichte über Handel und Industrie.*

Great Britain FO
  1873   *Report... respecting Factories for Spinning and Weaving of Textile Fabrics Abroad.* London.

Great Britain, Accounts and Papers.

———, Foreign Office.

Halep Vilayeti Salnamesi.

Herlt, G.
  1918   "Die Industrialisierung der Türkei," *Das Wirtschaftsleben der Türkei*, II.

İnalcık, Halil
  1979–
  1980   "Osmanlı Pamuklu Pazarı, Hindistan ve İngiltere: Pazar Rekabetinde Emek Maliyetinin Rolü," *Middle East Technical University Studies in Development*, Special Issue.

Issawi, Charles
  1982   *An Economic History of the Middle East and North Africa.* New York.

Issawi, Charles
  1988   *The Fertile Crescent 1800–1914. A Documentary Economic History.* New York.

Levant Trade Review.

Luckerts, I.
  1906   "Le développement industriel de la Turquie d'Asie," *Le Mouvement Économique*, 1 er Juin.

Nuri, Hifzi
  1922/
  1338   *Kayseri Sancağı.* Ankara.

Owen, Roger
  1981   *The Middle East in the World Economy.* London.

Pamuk, Şevket
  1987   *The Ottoman Empire and European Capitalism.* Cambridge.

Quataert, Donald
  1986   "Machine Breaking and the Changing Carpet Industry of Western Anatolia, 1860–1908," *Journal of Social History*, Spring.

Quataert, Donald
   1992   *Technology Transfer and Manufacturing in the Ottoman Empire, 1800–1914.* İstanbul.

Quataert, Donald
   1993b   *Ottoman Manufacturing in the Age of the Industrial Revolution.* Cambridge.

La Revue Commerciale du Levant.

Scherzer, K.von
   1873   *Smyrna.* Wein.

Selanik Vilayeti Salnamesi.

Sewell, William
   1980   *Work and Revolution in France.* Cambridge.

Sivas Vilayeti Salnamesi.

Stich, Heinrich
   1929   *Die Weltwirtschaftlich Entwicklung der Anatolischen Produktion seit Anfangs des 19. Jahrhunderts.* Keil.

Turkey
   1289–
   1302   *Düstur.*

Turkey
   1968   *Uşak İl Yıllığı 1967.* İstanbul.

Turkey
   1970   *Osmanlı Sanayii. 1913, 1915 Yılları Sanayi Istatistiki.* Ankara.

United States, National Archives.
        Consular Reports.
        Department of Commerce and Labor, Bureau of Manufacturing, *Turkey for 1907.*

Manufacturing in the Ottoman Empire and in Republican Turkey, ca. 1900–1950

Çağlar Keyder

This article analyzes manufacturing in the Ottoman Empire and Turkey during the transitional period between the two entities, i.e., roughly the first half of the twentieth century. Until 1950, the structuring of the manufacturing sector could be understood in terms of the historical particularity of the Ottoman social formation, its political and economic interaction with the world economy, and its dismantlement. After 1950, the pattern of manufacturing development became assimilated to a world-wide blueprint which applied to a set of countries with similar levels of social and economic transformation as Turkey. In other words, the historical genetic method of inquiry proves less revealing after World War II when the general contours of peripheral manufacturing development begin to dominate. Therefore, I will stop this analysis in 1950, as a new type of capitalist development begins to prevail. I will trace the evolution of manufacturing through the first half of the century by means of the following periodization: the war years (1912–1923), reconstruction

(1924–1929), economic crisis and etatism (1930–1939), and war and its aftermath. First, however, a short overview of the manufacturing structure inherited from the nineteenth century is in order.

THE NINETEENTH CENTURY HERITAGE

Three separate forms of manufacturing could be identified in the nineteenth century: small handicrafts, modern manufactures undertaken by the state, and privately owned urban manufactures of recent origin. Traditional small manufacture was found in large and small cities as well as the countryside. Its characteristic feature was the mobilization of small capital employing a primitive, labor-intensive technology with a traditional organization of labor. Often, the unit of production coincided with the household: workers consisted of the owner of the enterprise (the head of the household) and immediate family members. Hired labor, when it existed, was occluded in many ways: workers from outside could be living within the household or apprenticing with the master. Although a strict guild organization was no longer practiced by the end of the nineteenth century, some social dimensions of the Ottoman *lonca* and *gedik* survived.[1]

One significant transformation in small manufacturing had been its harnessing to the export trade during the later nineteenth century. The more prominent export-oriented sectors were organized in the putting-out system, where family labor depended on advances from a merchant.[2] The nature of labor use in the sector varied along a continuum: some households worked for merchants while some bought and sold on their own behalf. It is important to distinguish between merchant-controlled, export-oriented small manufactures and those catering to local consumption, because each is affected differently by economic conjuncture. A general decline in foreign trade would hurt the former but might benefit the latter.

Most small manufacturing catering to local markets managed to survive the competition of European imports. Although new orientations became available to this particular form of organizing labor, its survival essentially depended on the level and speed of import penetration into local markets. The effect of imports, however, was not always negative. While, for example, hand spinning as a commercial activity disappeared, hand loom production was stimulated by the easy availability of imported cotton thread. Both in its traditional forms where transportation difficulties or taste advantages helped stave off competition from imports, and in the newer export-oriented mode, external trade relations dominated the fate of small manufacturing. (See Quataert in this volume).

State-owned manufactures developed during the nineteenth century. In terms of technology and scale, they radically differed from the local norms and closely approximated industrial factory technology. This was no accident since the imitation of European factories was a conscious policy, often carried out through the importing of all necessary factors of production. There was a major difference, however: these manufactures were the product of state policy, designed to respond to demand originating in the palace and the military. The state mobilized the necessary capital through its own revenues or through foreign loans. Most of the managers and skilled workers were brought from abroad. The locally recruited unskilled workers were, at least initially, found among convicts, army conscripts, and from populations which were considered to be outside the integral structure of the Ottoman society.[3] The artificiality of this form of production quickly became evident in the rapid collapse of most of the enterprises. Raw material and labor imports could not easily be secured and machines could not be maintained. The turnover of the locally recruited workers was high; they were not trained properly, and there were frequent accidents. When imports became cheaper or demand conditions changed, the factories became redundant and were left to crumble. Nonetheless, a small number of these state enterprises survived into the twentieth century and were inherited by the Republic.

A third significant form of production which was organized in an overtly capitalist fashion also evolved during the latter part of the century. Its roots were in small manufacturing, but it was organized in an overtly capitalist fashion. This was urban manufacturing of varying scale catering to the expanding urban population of foreign and minority merchants, financiers, professionals, and the 'modernizing' segments of the Muslim elite. The port cities of İstanbul, Salonica, and İzmir, where trade was organized, were the privileged locales of this new intermediary population and, therefore, of the new form of manufacturing. The entrepreneurs were mostly Ottoman Greeks and Armenians or resident foreigners; most of the workers also were non-Muslims. Construction materials industry, printing, beverages, confectionery and patisserie, bottle making, paper, and iron foundries constituted examples of such activity. The scale of production often remained below ten workers per establishment. But the form of production represented by these enterprises was novel because of the introduction of the wage relation bringing together a proletarianized, free labor force and free capital, contracting freely in a labor market.[4]

The Ottoman Social Formation

Before I begin to elaborate on the trajectory of each of these forms of manufacturing production during the twentieth century, it will be useful to briefly talk about the specificity of the Ottoman/Turkish social formation towards the closing years of the empire. This discussion will serve to situate these forms and explain their relative weights.

Small peasant property was the rule in Ottoman Anatolia. With one very important regional exception that we will discuss later, large property in land did not emerge and accumulation on the basis of landownership remained improbable.[5] The eighteenth-century ascendancy of local potentates, that had intimated the emergence of a new landed gentry to share the (largely) agrarian surplus with the bureaucracy, had been reversed by the strengthening of central authority during the first half of the nineteenth century. Hence, large managed estates were not established in Anatolia and the independent family farm survived intact. By mid-nineteenth century the local potentates had disappeared from the scene and the role that they had played in the local economy was set to be taken over by a very different group of intermediaries.

Anatolia did become part of the nineteenth-century world economy, but its level of integration was relatively modest. During the fifty years following the re-opening of the Mediterranean to international commerce, Anatolian trade grew at respectable rates. After the 1860s, however, it stagnated.[6] This performance was due partly to the poor natural endowment of Anatolia; the real problem, however, was the pattern of land ownership. Since it proved impossible to consolidate large landholding through expropriation of the peasantry, it was difficult to find dependent peasants who would submit to the kind of exploitation that was common in Eastern Europe or Egypt. Hence, neither the pre-incorporation order itself, nor the changes imposed upon this order by integration into the world market led to a concentration of the agrarian surplus in a few hands. Without this concentration, investments to increase the volume and profitability of trade, such as in transportation or irrigation or in financing land reclamation and improvement, were not forthcoming either. There was, however, money to be made in the expanding commercial sector, notably through the new intermediary positions in trade and finance to collect the agrarian surplus, to channel it toward ports of export, and to supply the advance funds to induce peasants to switch to world-market crops. Imports also had to be purchased, distributed, and retailed. In an agrarian structure where surplus is concentrated, large landlords are often themselves merchants; they may establish more equal relationships with merchants or (as in most of eastern Europe) even subordinate them politically. In Anatolia, by contrast, the intermediary class formed outside of the agrarian economy itself, and by virtue of dealing with the peasantry (by definition powerless) obtained a superior position.

This intermediary class, at first subsidiary to foreign merchants, gradually became independent, and was successful in preventing direct control of the local economy by foreigners. There were a few 'Levantine' families, mostly of pre-nineteenth century origin, who continued to be active in finance and trade; but natives were the core of the new class. Foreign merchant houses and banks at first needed and used them; after ca. 1875, however, the Ottoman intermediary class was strong enough to undertake commercial and manufacturing investments in its own right. By the 1890s, this group clearly had become an independent bourgeoisie in Anatolia, bound neither to a landlord class nor to foreign capital.

Before the nineteenth century, the economic difference between Muslims and non-Muslims was not overwhelming (although there were proportionately more Christians involved in trade and lending.) With growing foreign trade Greeks and Armenians came to constitute the great majority of the intermediary class. Many factors played a role in this transformation. In addition to real or constructed cultural affinity, Capitulations had allowed foreign representatives to extend legal extraterritoriality to Ottoman subjects. As a result, non-Muslims could receive protected status from the European powers which effectively placed them beyond the reach of Ottoman law and Ottoman tax authorities. In effect, the multi-ethnic social structure of the Empire had prepared for an 'ethnic division of labor' that eventually culminated in a class differentiation.[7]

This new class was quantitatively large, precisely because the intermediation they performed was an extensive one that reached over a large number of producers each commanding a small amount of surplus. In all the large cities of trade, as well as in smaller towns on the road network, the nascent bourgeoisie of Greeks and Armenians began to live in refracted Western styles, adopting consumption patterns, cultural emoluments, and manners. The cumulative effect of economic success and changing life style came to radically divorce the non-Muslim populations from the prevailing norms in the empire.

We may now relate the three forms of manufacturing identified earlier to the social transformation of the empire. Small manufactures obviously were inherited from the less rapidly evolving and relatively closed structure of the traditional empire. They derived from the division of labor between town and country as well as from a rudimentary plan imposed on the economy by the state whose principal purpose was to provision the administrative centers. Their regulation under administrative control became weaker as the economy fell under external influences. With increasing foreign trade they were left at the mercy of the market.

State enterprises were the product of bureaucratic reformism. The bureaucracy was the ruling class of the classical order, collecting the agrarian surplus through taxation. As the expansion of the European economy threatened traditional balances, the bureaucracy responded with defensive maneuvers. They centralized the imperial administration in order to strengthen their rule, bolstered the military, and, as a corollary, founded state enterprises.

Finally, the new urban manufactures undertaken by the emerging bourgeoisie may be related to the transformation accompanying the incorporation of the empire into the world economy. This incorporation led to the formation of a numerically-strong intermediary class consisting of mainly non-Muslims. By the end of the century, the economic positioning of this intermediary class had changed: in addition to intermediation they began to engage in genuinely capitalist undertakings.[8] As the new urban life style and consumption pattern spread, so did the need for a rudimentary 'import substitution', the manufacture of the perceived necessities of the new life which were difficult or costly to import. Foreigners, Levantines, and local intermediaries invested in such manufacturing.

THE POLITICAL TRANSITION FROM EMPIRE TO REPUBLIC

The dissolution of the Ottoman Empire and the foundation of the Turkish Republic took place within the conditions defined by a nationalist movement. It was the state elite which felt that a non-Muslim class in ascendance threatened the traditional social structure, as well as the status of the bureaucracy itself.[9] Consequently, they adopted a nationalist position as they perceived the threat of nationalist, irredentist and separatist politics, coming from especially the Greek and Armenian communities. The structural reasons for a conflict between the Muslim bureaucracy representing the traditional social order and a non-Muslim bourgeoisie embracing the market and capitalist accumulation were certainly there. As nationalist attitudes were gradually diffused to the population at large, widespread ethnic hostility resulted.

By the advent of the Constitutional regime in 1908, despite the temporary euphoria and dreams of coexistence under the mantle of a reformed empire, conflict between the Muslims and non-Muslims had become frequent, and a demand for Islamization, if not yet Turkification, was emerging. The later Committee of Union and Progress (CUP) governments, especially after the Balkan wars, used ethnic conflict to legitimate their power. In settling Muslim immigrants from the Balkans, arranging boycotts of imported goods, and orchestrating strikes, they sent an unmistakable message to the Greek and Armenian populations that their presence and status would not be tolerated as before. As positive policy, the CUP initiated conscious measures of promoting Muslim business through government contracts and subsidies. This policy did not bear fruit until the war years when the government instituted a more planned war economy. Another significant policy of the war years was the unilateral abrogation of the Capitulations, an act which abolished the fiscal and legal advantages enjoyed by foreign passport holders.[10]

Most crucially, however, Islamization proceeded on the basis of the physical removal of the non-Muslim population. Starting in 1909, when they were conscripted into the army for the first time, there had been a steady emigration of Greeks and Armenians. During the war, this trend accelerated. In 1915, the Armenian population of most of the interior regions was officially deported, leading to a large number of deaths. During the War of Liberation (1919–22) a civil war ensued where Armenians and Greeks perished and were driven out of their homes. When Turkish forces defeated the Greek army in 1922, some half a million Greeks fled to Greece; finally, in the exchange of populations agreed upon in the Lausanne Peace Conference, the remaining Greek Orthodox population, excepting those who were legally residents of the city of İstanbul, were forced to emigrate. By 1924, less than one-tenth of the non-Muslim population of 1908 (around 2.5 million) remained in the new Republic.[11] This population movement had formidable social consequences in addition to drastically changing the ethnic composition of the new Republic. First, most of the bourgeoisie, especially those in cities other than İstanbul, had disappeared. There was, however, no Muslim-Turkish bourgeoisie waiting in the wings to take over from the departing Christians. A social vacuum resulted whose peculiar rectification defined the political and ideological problems, which continuously haunted Turkish society during the Republican period. Secondly, the political class that had organized and led the war against invading armies, carried the nationalist banner, and became the benefactor of all the groups who stood to gain from the expulsion of Greeks and Armenians, emerged from the conflict unchallenged. This class charted the course of the new Turkish Republic with a great deal of autonomy. Thirdly, government policies and the weakness of the potential Turkish bourgeoisie resulted in an expanded role for foreign capital that, to some extent, substituted for the managerial and entrepreneurial experience lost during the war years.[12] Until the 1930s depression, foreign capital played a significant role in the reconstruction of the urban manufacturing sector.

MANUFACTURING DURING THE TRANSITION PERIOD

We may now discuss the implications of the above propositions for the course of manufacturing and the fortunes of the three types identified earlier.

a) Local-market-oriented small manufactures performed badly during the 1920s. Reconstruction and involvement of foreign capital led to rapid increases in agricultural production and exports. In fact, despite a smaller population, export revenues in some products such as tobacco and cotton reached their pre-war levels by the mid-1920s. Foreign merchants dispensing generous export credits became particularly active and, as a result, the rural population in the more commercialized regions experienced rapidly increasing incomes.[13] Thus, greater specialization in agriculture occurred at the expense of Z-good activities, because of a smaller population and high returns in agriculture. Peace and prosperity after a decade of war also must have increased the propensity to substitute imported, fancier wares for the traditional products of domestic industry and small manufactures. Anecdotal evidence suggests that Muslim peasants were introduced to imported consumables during the 1920s, which explains the poor performance of local small manufacturing.

Small manufacturing in rural areas (whether local market or export oriented) is an activity employing essentially agricultural labor. Post-war Anatolian agriculture was lucrative and offered relatively high returns precisely because it was characterized by a labor shortage and land abundance. The government tried to counteract the scarcity of labor by issuing decrees that townsmen should participate in agrarian production, that neighbors should help cultivate widows' lands, etc. In other words, although Anatolian land/labor ratios had steadily declined during the second half of the previous century, they remained, in the 1920s, less than conducive to labor-intensive, low-wage manufacturing activity.

Small manufacturing had its origins in the traditional structure of the society, and it catered mostly to small towns and richer rural areas. One component of it, exemplified in cotton textiles, was the most sensitive to competition from imported manufactures, and it became clear during the 1920s and 1930s that there was a negative correlation between the availability of imports and cotton cloth manufacturing on unmechanized looms. It was estimated that there were around 100,000 weavers in the late 1930s, when imports were curtailed, up from a third as much in the 1920s.[14]

Cotton textiles, tanneries, leather manufactures, and iron foundries were undertaken mostly by Muslim craftsmen. Certain artisanal activities had expanded during the nineteenth century—especially those considered the preserve of the Armenians: for example, metal working, masonry, and jewelery. In any multi-ethnic society such divisions of labor are common, and the summary expulsion of one of the ethnic groups in the society predictably resulted in a long period of transition, if not permanent loss of the common store of industrial skill and experience. In fact, Republican Turkey, and in particular the cities of Anatolia, suffered from the loss of Armenian artisanship for at least a generation. By the time per capita income (and presumably demand patterns) attained their pre-war levels, the transferable knowledge had been lost and cheap substitutes had been found for most of the products in question. This particular loss could have been a factor in the often remarked absence of Turkish entrepreneurs of artisanal origin.[15] It may be that artisanal ranks supplied some of the entrepreneurs in import-substituting urban manufacturing during the Ottoman era. Or, perhaps there was a productive articulation between the two forms, leading to a strong foundation for industrial development.[16] However realized or substantial this potential, the post-war Turkish economy no longer contained it.

Finally, as mentioned above, the nineteenth century had witnessed a reorientation of some domestic manufacturing toward exports. Carpets and silk were the two most significant, both putting-out activities, although there were, at various times, other sectors that met European demand for the product of nimble fingers.[17] Most of these fields of manufacturing activity were organized by foreign or minority merchants. In some, for example silk, the labor force was also predominantly non-Muslim.[18] Greek merchants who left Anatolia and settled in Greece after 1923 found it easy to substitute Greek for Anatolian labor and successfully out-competed Anatolian exports in the world market.[19] In the case of carpets and silk, pre-war levels were never re-attained once the Greeks and the Armenians had left. In many cities in the Aegean region, houses, warehouses, and workshops remained empty, mainly because the departing population was not totally replaced. (The population of Anatolia during the 1920s was smaller, less urban, less commercialized, and certainly poorer than during the pre-war era.[20] Immigration from Russia, the Balkans, and Greece had compensated for war-time losses to some degree and the 1920s situation was less disastrous than would have been.[21])

I will briefly recount the collapse of the silk industry after the war as a paradigmatic case that reveals many of the features of the transition.[22] Starting in Winter, 1912, CUP-organized boycotts against Greek business had intensified. At around the same time, increasing numbers of Muslims from areas occupied by Greece started to arrive in Turkey, and were settled in western Anatolia, mostly in regions where there had been significant concentrations of Greeks. The boycott did not remain confined to commercial centers and soon evolved into attacks against Greek villages to the west of Bursa. Most Greek farmers who were driven out were silk producers. They abandoned their farms and mulberry trees, which subsequently were destroyed. In August 1915, Armenian deportations took place. Armenian villagers of the Bursa region were also silk growers and filature owners. The newly arriving immigrant Muslims who occupied the abandoned farms and villages were not at all familiar with silk growing. As a result, mulberry trees were made into firewood and food grains and tobacco planted in their place. By 1921, the war with occupying Greek forces had destroyed some of the remaining silkworm growing centers in the environs of Bursa and led anew to the emigration of the skilled labor force.

As a result of wartime destruction, production in the Bursa region declined from over four million kg of cocoons in 1913 to 810,000 kg in 1919. In 1922, the total was around 300,000 kg. In March 1920, two-thirds of the 150 filatures, which had existed in Bursa province in 1914, had been destroyed because of theft, pillage, and government requisitioning. The Bursa silk-weaving industry ordinarily absorbed 25 to 30,000 kg of raw silk annually but, in 1921, only one-fifth of this quantity was required. At the same time, hand weaving of silk cloth had declined to one-fourth of the former level.

After the arrival of peace, various schemes were proposed to revive the silk industry, such as instructing the new inhabitants of the region in silk worm cultivation and subsidizing the planting of new mulberry trees. The government of the new Republic convened meetings in Bursa to discuss the state of the silk industry, but there was only a small revival and Turkey lost its once significant position in the world silk market.[23] A similar fate overtook all the export-oriented manufactures which had developed during the nineteenth century. In all of them there were sharp reversals; some did briefly recover in the 1920s, but the economic depression blocked restoration of previous levels of production.

b) The second form of manufacturing we have considered did not receive much attention during the transition from empire to republic. Nevertheless, in 1914, there were 5,000 workers in state factories, some two-thirds in military provisioning.[24] During the war, there was growing need for military supplies and the bottleneck seemed to be the scarcity of labor. Various schemes were devised in order to insure its supply. One project, in particular, met with success: the employment of women in Istanbul factories deemed important for the war effort.[25] By the end of the war, however, state enterprises again were eclipsed. During the initial years of the republic, the bureaucracy was not yet in a position to invest in state manufacturing. There were rebellions against the new government, factional strife within the ruling group, and widespread hostility to its social reform programs. During this period of reconstruction, with its ready supply of foreign capital and credit, large profits awaited all who could step in to fill the gap left by the casualties of external and internal wars. Hence, state enterprise took no part in the reconstruction effort until the 1930s, when it became the principal instrument of the state-led industrialization effort. Only during the 1930s Depression, and with Soviet and fascist examples in view, was state enterprise accorded an essential role.

c) The growth of state enterprise had not been one of the objectives of the Young Turk regime because its economic nationalism was based more on Listian *dirigisme* than etatism. When the Young Turks came to power, their overarching objective seemed to be the nurturing of a Muslim bourgeoisie.[26] Hence, their efforts concentrated on the third form of urban, import-substituting manufacturing production which held the greatest potential in terms of the transfer of economic power to a Muslim bourgeoisie. This emphasis implied that Muslim businessmen were supported, given incentives, and subsidized by the government. The share of Muslim ownership in capitalist enterprise no doubt increased significantly during the War but this Islamization was due principally to the departure and expulsion of the Christian bourgeoisie. The policy of promoting and encouraging Muslim businessmen constituted the major legacy of the CUP government to the Republicans. In fact, at the end of the war and throughout the 1920s, the Republican political elite were not enthusiastic about expanding the purview of the public sector; the successful takeover of existing enterprises by Turks seemed to be their principal concern.

The reconstruction of the 1920s largely depended on the success of Turkish businessmen in taking over the third type of urban manufacturing left behind by the departing bourgeoisie. Industrial production had almost disappeared toward the end of the war, only to be somewhat boosted by consumption demand of the Occupation forces after 1919. Nevertheless, investment in industry was negligible during 1919–1923.[27] With peace, Turkish merchants, after 1923, were surprisingly successful in recovering the pre-war levels of agricultural exports; their success in manufacturing, however, remained limited. The example of manufacturing in İzmir may illuminate some of the problems involved.

İzmir was the second most prosperous city in the pre-war empire. Its population included Greeks, Jews, Armenians, foreigners, and Levantines as well as Muslims who constituted a plurality; but the Greek minority justifiably regarded the city as under Hellenic cultural and economic domination. When Greece entered the war, there had been reprisals on the Ottoman Greeks, and informal pressure to accept Turkish partnership in their businesses. Greek businessman accepted relatives of high officials as fictitious partners. Thus, a foreign or Greek company became "Turkish" and escaped confiscation. This particular Turkification, however, was short-lived. Under Greek occupation, Ottoman Greek manufacturers were given back their factories, and they asked for and received compensation for losses suffered during the war. Under Greek occupation, İzmir businessmen gained greater autonomy than before, having been liberated from the bureaucratic control of the Ottoman governor. The following tables and descriptions are from a report on manufacturing in the İzmir region prepared for the National Bank of Greece in 1920, under orders from the occupation authority.[28] There may be a bias in the account toward establishing a stronger Greek presence than was the case. The peace conferences were still in progress, and such accounts were thought to weigh heavily in the deliberations. Nonetheless, these figures seem valuable.

Table 4 Number of Industrial Establishments in İzmir by Nationality of Ownership

Greek	4,002	Austrian	6
Turkish	1,216	Italian	3
Armenian	28	American	2
Jewish	21	German	2
British	13	Belgian	1
French	8		

Source: Trakakis Report.

Table 5 Greek and Turkish Major Industrial Establishments that were in Operation in 1920. Listed by Date of Establishment and Ownership

Date of Establishment	Greek	Turkish
1800–30	18	1
1831–50	27	1
1851–60	36	2
1861–70	59	2
1871–80	92	10
1881–90	177	19
1891–00	239	43
1901–10	241	17
1911–19	91	22

Source: Trakakis Report (excludes domestic industry and water mills and other small plants).

The report claims that ninety-five percent of the workers in the city of İzmir were Greeks (both Ottoman and Greek subjects), while in the Aydin province overall, the figure was seventy-six percent. Manufacturing workers in the province totalled 37,000, fifteen percent of whom were Turks. According to the report Muslim workers were employed mostly as porters and in tanneries owned by Muslims. In the smaller towns of the interior, they worked in rope manufacturing and in mines. Muslim women worked in fig packing, in patisserie factories, in the raisin trade, in the two spinning mills, and in knitting socks and flannels. The slight Turkish presence makes clear that Turkification and economic reconstruction would be a very difficult task.

As examples of the form of manufacturing which catered to urban demand, was import-substituting, and employed free urban workers, we may cite some examples from the report.

- Flour mills: all but one were owned by Greeks, and employed close to 300 workers.
- Breweries: this industry was entirely monopolized by one factory, a branch of Swiss Brasseries Réunies Bomonti-Nectar, which also ran two factories in İstanbul. The company was established in 1911 by Swiss investors, subsequently some local Greeks who wanted to form a rival firm were incorporated into Bomonti and given partnerships. It employed forty workers and supplied the interior of Anatolia, the islands of Samos and Lesbos, as well as other parts of the Aydın vilayet.

- Beverages: there were four factories in İzmir, two Greek, one Swiss, one Muslim owned, that manufactured carbonated drinks. There were also smaller factories operating in Bergama, Ayvalık, Manisa, and Aydın.
- Wine making: there were 174 manufacturers of every scale in the İzmir area—all Greek. The market was entirely local.
- Alcohol distilling: this industry developed during the war as a result of import difficulties. Some forty-five distilleries were established (forty-four Greek and one Turkish) but soon after the armistice they ceased operations due to imports of cheap American alcohol. There was also a liqueur manufacturing activity, entirely Greek.
- Soap making: there were eleven soap manufacturers in İzmir, five in Aydın, and numerous small factories elsewhere in the province. In İzmir, two of the smaller factories were owned by Muslims, the rest by Greeks.
- Leather: tanning was dominated by Muslim businessmen, although two Greek factories stood out due to modern technology and quality. There were 150 workers in the major tanneries, and more in the fifteen to twenty smaller Muslim owned establishments. The authorities requisitioned the Greek owned tanneries as soon as the war broke out, only two could rescue their machinery by taking Muslims as partners. The rest received compensation from İstanbul after the armistice.
- Pastry: there were ten to twelve pastry factories, entirely dominated by Greeks. They were supplied by big Greek merchants importing sugar from Trieste and Russia.
- Gaslight: the gaslight company was British owned, operating from a concession granted in 1859. It was inadequate in lighting İzmir, however, and many small and profitable electricity generating plants had been established by local investors.

While this brief description of the conditions of manufacturing in İzmir may overstate Greek domination of the economy, it clearly does suggest the difficulties involved in nationalization. When the entire Greek population departed, there was neither a class of Muslim businessmen nor a proletariat to fill all the slots vacated. It is true that in some cities of the interior Muslim businessmen had dominated manufacturing. Two things should be remembered, however. First, most of the industry was in the western region of Turkey: in İstanbul, İzmir, and Bursa; and Greeks were in heavy concentration in these cities.[29] These three cities accounted for fifty-five percent, twenty-five percent, and five percent, respectively, of all the manufacturing value added in industry (excluding small manufactures) before 1914.[30] Second, even in the interior cities Greeks and Armenians were economically important to a disproportionate extent. In fact, only twenty percent of all the enterprises enumerated in the incomplete 1913–1915 census were Muslim-owned.[31] Hence, there was a considerable vacuum left in the manufacturing sector as a result of the ethnic cleansing of the country. As suggested above, both the CUP government, pursuing the policy specifically, and the Republican government, as part of a larger reconstruction effort, sought to fill this vacuum.

Paradoxically, the departure of the native non-Muslim bourgeoisie left the field open to foreign capital. Turkish businessmen played a subordinate role in the reconstruction process. While the bourgeoisie of the Ottoman period had attained, by the end of the previous century, the strength to defend their autonomy against foreign capitalists, the Republican bourgeoisie was too inexperienced. Foreign capital accounted for sixty-seven percent of the investment in manufacturing corporations in the 1920s.[32] In other words, foreign capital in manufacturing corporations was double the amount of Turkish capital. This figure, of course, would be smaller if investment in all manufacturing (including small manufactures that were not, in general, corporations) could be measured. About one-fourth of the foreign capital was invested in municipal utilities, then, in decreasing importance, came four cement plants, and three companies in food processing. The overall importance of foreign capital was due to large scale investments. In each sector the number of foreign companies was small but capital invested in each was several times that of Turkish companies.[33]

Foreign capital corporations often had local partners who were Levantines. But the crucial tie to the new regime was supplied by one or more silent partners who presumably shared in the profits but only lent their names to the board of directors in order to legitimate the enterprise. Unsurprisingly, these silent partners in the larger corporations invariably were deputies of the new Parliament.

THE REPUBLIC DURING THE 1920s

This reconstruction, characterized by a native class of businessmen endeavoring to replace an ousted bourgeoisie, lasted for only a brief period. The abrupt interruption was due to the world economic crisis. Had the economic conjuncture of the 1920s continued for another decade, Turkish merchants and industrialists, especially in the provinces, might have come of age and reproduced some of the economic, social, and cultural accomplishments of the non-Muslim bourgeoisie of the pre-war era.

The attempt at reconstruction was a qualified success. In 1927, for example, there was a thirty percent increase in the number of work places as compared to 1921; and a sixty percent increase in the number of workers in manufacturing.[34] These figures are significant because they cover manufacturing outside of the large centers of İstanbul, İzmir and Bursa. The 1921 census was conducted in the area under the control of the Ankara government, and therefore excluded the occupied cities and regions where most of the manufacturing capacity was located. Hence, the increase calculated here, although from a low point in 1921, is a good guide for economic reconstruction in the provinces.[35] Again, according to the 1927 census, there were 65,245 plants in Turkey employing 256,855 workers. Of these, 3,522 plants were found in İzmir province.[36] In other words, if we make a heroic assumption of comparability, it would seem that out of the 5,300 İzmir manufacturing plants in 1920 (see Table 4), the absolute loss had been only 1,800 plants. Even more optimistic is the conclusion that while there were only 1,300 non-Greek plants in 1920, in 1927 their number had increased to 3,500. The reconstruction of the 1920s lasted a brief period. With the advent of the economic crisis after 1929, the development stopped.

THE CRISIS OF THE 1930s

The economic crisis arrived in Turkey through the payments mechanism. Inflows of foreign capital and merchant credit had been financing a growing trade deficit that originated in increasing demand for manufactures. Within the import bill, however, the share of investment and intermediate goods had been increasing, indicating that economic reconstruction permitting the satisfaction of pent-up consumer demand also was accompanied by imports feeding into manufacturing production. By 1929, imports were 284 million turkish lira (TL) while exports remained at 190 million TL, and the flow of short-term credit was about to end.[37] The abrupt fall in demand for Turkey's agricultural exports and the deteriorating terms of trade added to the problem. By the end of 1929, a crisis mentality already had taken hold of both foreign and Turkish businessmen. From the point of view of the reconstruction of the Turkish economy, it was a disaster that the crisis arrived only six years after peace.

First hit were the export and import merchants who had overextended themselves on the assumption that foreign credit would continue to underwrite their operations. Various larger firms connected with external trade followed suit. Net inflows of foreign capital ceased with the collapse of the world market; the government nationalized some former investments such as railroads and more recent investments were liquidated. Foreign businessmen disappeared from the scene fearing that the larger manufacturing corporations established recently would also be liquidated. In 1931, press reports in İstanbul claimed 100,000 workers were unemployed.[38]

Coincidentally, the free trade regime that the government had seen no reason to dispute in the Lausanne peace conference also came to an end in 1929; to be replaced by a relatively protectionist one. Following the worldwide trend, high duties were imposed on imported manufactures, drastically changing the terms of trade against agriculture. Cheap food and unemployment drove wages down. The new conditions favoring manufacturing led to rudimentary import substitution in İstanbul work-shops where former importers profitably turned to the finishing of imported raw materials. This new activity, however, hardly compensated for the demise of larger manufacturing that had been fueled by foreign capital. Nonetheless, from the point of view of accumulation in private hands, it prepared for a certain investment potential that was realized later. Joint-stock companies were in bad shape during 1929 and 1930, either losing money or earning a very small positive rate on paid-up capital.[39] By contrast, smaller concerns set up to benefit from the new protectionist regime were doing very well. Shacks that housed a handful of workers, drawing wire to make nails for example, were suddenly glorified and called 'factories', and their owners earned huge profits.[40] Presumably the older corporations were overly dependent on imported inputs, and were identified strongly with the ownership patterns of the previous period. They do not seem to have been successful in making the transition.

This conclusion is supported by a functional differentiation that can be observed in the later period. Joint-stock companies of the 1920s usually had Levantines, Greeks, and Armenians on their boards, sitting together with representatives of the new Republican elite.[41] The 1930s did not witness the elimination of the Levantines and the İstanbul Christians from the business world. Their participation in manufacturing, however, declined and they began to specialize almost exclusively in trade. They continued to be active in foreign commerce and in representing foreign firms. In the imperial economy, their social orientation had provided a modernizing example. Now, both from the point of view of the direction that the economy had taken, and in terms of their social and political impact, this group became thoroughly marginal.

The Turkish businessmen, now coalesced around the new seat of power, took their position in the economic world. Most of them owed their initial impetus to CUP policies, and some had benefited from the property distribution after the war. The Republican government implemented two measures that directly helped their accumulation process. One was a legislation entitled Encouragement of Industry. This law, first promulgated in 1913, was revised in 1927. It provided tax exemptions, eased importing inputs, and promised government purchases and other incentives to be accorded to manufacturing investments exceeding certain scale requirements. In 1932, some 1,473 manufacturing companies (690 in İstanbul and İzmir) benefited from the incentives supplied through this legislation. The average number of workers in these companies was thirty-eight; they were relatively mechanized with an average use of seventy horsepower per plant.[42] In the 1927 census, the average number of workers in all manufacturing plants had been 3.9, and mechanical power used 0.6 horsepower.[43] The second measure was more specific and perhaps more effective in the case of bigger entrepreneurs. It involved the formation, less than a year after the Republic itself, of a semi-official but seemingly private bank designed to extend credit to private manufacturing. Its founders and shareholders were Mustafa Kemal, the President of the Republic, high officials of the government, deputies, and officially recognized merchants. Its president was the former Minister of the Economy. Manufacturing was predictably and perennially short of long-term capital, and the new Bank of Business (İş Bankası) was supposed to rectify the situation. Although initially oriented to the commercial sector, it eventually succeeded in becoming an investment bank for private industry. Because of its close relations with the government and its uniqueness in the field, it also became an exceptionally effective planning agency whose services were avidly sought during the 1930s. During the 1920s, the Bank of Business was the only large 'private' bank with a significant number of depositors whose directors were Turkish. These directors sat on the boards of the largest of private manufacturing concerns and they served in the Parliament and in the higher echelons of the bureaucracy. The bank served as the medium of the formation of a new nexus between the bureaucracy and business. In

1930, its participation in industry had grown to fifty percent of all national banks.[44] Since deputies and the higher administrative personnel doubled as businessmen, and as the İstanbul bourgeoisie recognized that the new economy was mediated through decrees and dicta issued from Ankara, a slow merger began to occur between the older and the newer bourgeoisie and the new governing class. The Business Bank emerged as the private sector pole in this merger. To be sure, there were disputes as to the mix between the realm of the private and the public, but no radical modification of the balance.

STATE PLANNING AND MANUFACTURING DURING THE 1930s

Within three years of the 1929 crisis, the Ankara government had prepared an interventionist economic program with an anti-liberal rhetoric. After 1932, the government gradually fashioned the instruments of intervention that made it possible to implement macro-economic policy.[45] At the same time, more direct management at the sectoral level became an aspiration especially since producers were willing to go along with labor control, price setting, and market division schemes, which apparently were inspired by the Italian example. As the economic crisis deepened, however, the more radical and interventionist wing of the ruling party argued that state enterprises had to be strengthened in order to achieve the goal of autarky. It should be stressed that such a program did not require radical organizational innovation. Some state enterprises dating from the nineteenth century were still in existence and a state bank (*Sanayi ve Maadin Bankası*) providing credit to state enterprises was already in operation. The major state-owned factories still in existence were two textile plants and a leather-working plant in İstanbul, a cloth-weaving plant in Ankara, one cotton yarn factory in İsparta, a sugar mill in Uşak, carpet manufactories in Hereke and Kayseri, and a ceramic factory in Kütahya. These had evolved from provisioning the army to producing basic consumer items such as coarse cloth, sturdy shoes, and sugar for the local market as well as traditional export items such as silk carpets and hand-painted tiles.

The proximate model for the new generation of state enterprises derived from the Soviet experience. This was not surprising because, in the worldwide anti-liberal atmosphere, Turkish bureaucrats did not distinguish between the Italian and the Soviet model, lauding both experiments despite their protests that they had no affinity with either fascism or bolshevism. Accordingly, a five-year plan of manufacturing investments was prepared comprising some twenty-one projects in textiles, iron and steel, ceramics and glass, paper, artificial fibres, and chemicals.[46] This plan became the blueprint of etatist industrialization during the subsequent years.[47]

The funding for the projects in the five-year plan derived essentially from the central government budget and from the Business Bank, but two loans were secured as well, from the Soviet government (eight million dollars gold) and from private sources in the United States (American-Turkish Investment Corporation—ten million dollars).[48] Another credit of ten million pounds was extended by the British in 1937, toward the construction of the steel works.[49] The projects proceeded swiftly: by the end of the plan period, most had been completed and were already in the production stage. The choice of projects had been guided by the objective of import substitution; thus one commentator at the time estimated that the sectors represented in the plan accounted for forty-three percent of Turkey's imports.[50] It certainly was true that cotton textiles, for instance, responded to an immediate consumption demand; and, since cotton was produced and ginned in the country, combined spinning and weaving mills would be technologically and economically feasible. With iron and steel, as well, there was a ready domestic market. The location of the plant, however, distant both from the source of iron ore and of coal, was chosen largely for military reasons. Military concerns determined the location of some of the other projects as well.[51]

State enterprises were on a much larger scale than private manufacturing. Larger amounts of capital could be mobilized, and the imported technology often required the employment of thousands. Surprisingly, these factories were located in small- and medium-size towns where there was no labor market to speak of. In fact, İstanbul and İzmir (and perhaps Adana) were the only cities where there were 'free' workers who constituted a 'supply' of labor in the market.[52] In Anatolian towns, every person was an owner—mostly of land but also of artisanal shops, small retail stores, etc. There had been no dispossession, and the population losses of the previous two decades had probably increased the incidence of ownership. When new state enterprises were located in such small towns of 20,000 to 50,000 in population, a work force had to be created *de novo*. Some workers were former craftsmen, but most found in factory employment a complementary source of income to their earnings as petty commodity producers. By contrast, private investment during the same period continued to be attracted by İstanbul and İzmir where there were both consumers and a labor market. The private sector was responsible for the increase in the share of the industrial labor force found in these two cities—from twenty-six percent in 1927 to thirty-three percent in 1950.[53]

Workers in the new state enterprises in smaller towns were characterized by absenteeism, high turnover, an absence of and/or resistance to work discipline. This was the cost paid for government policies that already had suppressed workers' movements during the political turmoil of the 1920s, and had, in 1936, passed a law reminiscent of fascist labor legislation. Dispersing the newly created industrial capacity, which employed the greatest concentration of workers, and employing workers who did not pose any threat of unionization or political activism were means of blocking the creation of a working class while promoting accumulation.

State industrialization was a success in terms of its contribution to manufacturing output and employment. Net national product increased by 5.2 percent per annum between 1933 and 1938; in 1950 there were 76,000 workers employed in 103 state manufacturing enterprises.[54] It was also a success in that it did not alienate the private sector. The top reaches of the bourgeoisie had no reason to challenge the state elite whose industrialization program opened up new fields of investment for them and did not compete with potential projects that could be financed privately. Etatism did not interfere with private accumulation. Under a strictly controlled trade regime (and later within the war economy) import permits, government contracts, and complementary production for military needs yielded visibly higher profits than manufacturing concerns. Even for the bourgeoisie who wanted to invest in manufacturing, state enterprises did not constitute a threat because they produced either intermediate inputs or consumption goods for the low end of the market, where profits were never as high as in luxury products.[55] The bloc consisting of the state elite, and the bourgeoisie organized around the state and the state banks, remained dominant until 1945. They benefited from general protectionism, specific incentive measures, external economies yielded by public enterprises, and government contracts.[56]

It is evident that the momentum of industrialization during the 1930s was supplied by the state sector while the private sector, whose rapid accumulation during the 1920s had been responsible for economic reconstruction, now continued to operate as an adjunct to the state sector. Of the total manufacturing investment of 190 million TL between 1933 and 1940, the public sector was responsible for 135 million, and the private for 55 million TL.[57] The fate of small manufacturing was more varied. The economic crisis had caused a return to rural and domestic industry and to the consumption of local manufactures.[58] In the cotton cloth manufacturing region of Denizli, for instance, the number of looms increased from 4,000 in 1927 to 8,000 in 1938.[59] Some of the recently introduced imported manufactures were given up in favor of locally produced items (imports declined from a high of 256m TL in 1929 to an average 80m TL in 1933–35).[60] On the other hand, export-oriented domestic manufacturing suffered yet another blow. Wool carpet exports declined from a 1,500,000 kg peak in 1928 to 200,000 kg in 1935. Carpet weaving in western Anatolia declined from an estimated 6,600 looms in 1927 to 2,500 looms in 1935.[61]

One estimate indicates that the volume of artisanal and small production increased by only ten percent from 1929 to 1939, while the index of total industrial production doubled. By the later date, state industry accounted for one-fourth of total manufacturing production, and employed 43,800 workers; hence, it was largely responsible for the increase.[62] A 1927 census counted 256,855 persons in manufacturing (excluding those working at home), working in 65,845 enterprises.[63] There was no census until 1950, when manufacturing employment was found to be 353,994, with 98,828 enterprises (again excluding home industry).[64] The coverage of these two censuses is not the same and they are not strictly comparable. We may, however, conjecture some comparisons. One, it would seem that state industry was the principal new manufacturing employment source during the 1930s and the private manufacturing sector lagged behind. Two, the lower average number of workers per enterprise indicates that a large number of very small plants (in addition to increasing numbers of persons involved in home industry that these figures do not cover) were started during these years, since state enterprises generally employed more than 100 workers each.[65]

ENTREPRENEURS IN THE PRIVATE SECTOR

In addition to the bureaucracy itself and the entrepreneurial bloc oriented to Ankara, there were two identifiable groups that managed to survive while remaining relatively distant from the center. Their survival, while in itself significant, also constituted a potential for taking over the accumulation momentum if and when the world context changed to prevent the statist alliance from leading the industrialization project. One was the Salonica *dönme* group in İstanbul. They were a culturally distinct group, boasting a tradition of capitalist experience and willingness to put themselves forth as candidates for a Turkish bourgeoisie. Along with other Muslim businessmen, they had arrived in İstanbul after Salonica had been annexed to Greece in 1912 and in 1923–24, during the exchange of populations. Salonica was the third largest economic center in the non-Arab regions of the Empire, and the part played by Muslim businessmen in its prosperity might have been relatively larger than in İstanbul or İzmir. Wealthy Salonicans indeed could serve as the core of a new bourgeois class. The *dönmes* enjoyed one more advantage, a special cohesiveness deriving from membership in a religious sect. They were followers of Sabbatai Zevi, the Jewish 'false prophet' of the seventeenth century who apostatized and ostensibly accepted Islam when threatened with execution. His followers had settled in Salonica, becoming important businessmen in the nineteenth century, especially active in the textile trade. More than their counterparts in other cities of the empire, they also had adopted the bourgeois lifestyle then usual in a Balkan, sub-metropole like Salonica. Upon their arrival in Turkey, they sought to reproduce some of the institutions of this lifestyle, notably a newspaper, journals, two secondary schools, clubs, and masonic lodges. They also invested in textiles and related manufacturing. Salonican families were successful during the 1920s, but when the center of gravity shifted from İstanbul to Ankara they remained socially aloof from the newly emerging alliance.[66]

The second group, which built its activity on an autonomous base, was vulnerable to but essentially independent from state intervention and favoritism. This was the large landlords of Çukurova (Cilicia), growing cotton for the most part, who invested in the usual forward linkages associated with cotton agriculture: ginning, cotton-seed oil processing, spinning, and weaving cloth. The presence of large landlords accumulating sufficient surpluses to make the transition to industry, in a social structure otherwise dominated by small-ownership, requires explanation. Unusually, the Adana area was characterized by large landholding. Its contours had much to do with İbrahim Pasha (Mehmed Ali's son) introducing cotton cultivation and seasonal labor when the region was under Egyptian occupation. As marshland was reclaimed and new settlements progressed, land came to be appropriated in large scale, both by newly settled tribal chiefs and merchants from the cities. The cotton famine stimulated a boom and contributed to the accumulation of wealth and land. By the end of the century, rich Christian (mostly Armenian) merchants and some Muslims owned large units.

Armenians and Greeks left the area during the war. Armenians returned under French occupation but departed in 1921 when the Turkish army reoccupied the region. The departure of Armenian landlords further boosted the concentration of land. During the 1920s and 1930s, Adana became an active business center, attractive to entrepreneurs.[67] The original accumulation permitted by cotton agriculture and by the appropriation of manufacturing plants created a regional economy which was initially export-oriented, but turned inward during the 1930s.

Already in 1914, the Çukurova region accounted for one-third of the value created by cotton textile plants. There were 5,000 workers employed in cotton textiles in 1914.[68] There were four large factories, three of which, owned by Christians, subsequently changed hands. Two of these acquired the same name, *Çukurova Mensucat*, although with different owners, while one had become National Textiles (*Milli Mensucat*); the fourth originally belonged to a Muslim businessman and did not change ownership.[69] The bourgeoisie developing in the Adana region was relatively immune to the Ankara-dominated public-private nexus, precisely because their wealth was based in land. At least three of the family 'holding companies' that were created in the 1950s and that now control a significant share of the modern sector in Turkish industry, originated in the Çukurova region. Their "primitive accumulation" could be traced to the 1920s.

THE WARTIME ECONOMY

The national income declined by two to three percent per annum during the war. In 1945, per capita income probably was below the levels of the late 1920s.[70] Most of the decline was due to the downturn in agriculture that suffered labor shortages and extortionary taxation.[71] The private manufacturing sector also confronted difficulties because of problems in securing inputs. But the picture was not entirely grim: the government increased its purchases and contracts, exports increased while civilian imports declined, creating new opportunities for manufacturers. An inept policy of compulsory agricultural sales and price controls led the way to black-market profiteering by provincial merchants. This latter group illegally provisioned the cities with government-rationed food items and accumulated large fortunes. Some merchants selling food and raw materials to Germany or purchasing arms for the government made huge profits which were subsequently invested in manufacturing. At the same time, however, imports of capital goods had to be curbed; the second industrialization plan was abandoned and the pace of government investment in manufacturing declined. Generally, there was a more strict application of the principles of etatism as state enterprises received privileged treatment. The Law for the Encouragement of Industry which accorded tax exemptions to the private sector was suspended and a new transactions tax was instituted to apply to all manufacturing.[72] One million men were drafted into the army even though Turkey stayed out of the War.

There was a general shortage of goods and a typical war economy based on rationing emerged. In textiles, for example, although both state and private industry had increased production rapidly during the previous period, twenty-five to thirty percent of yarn and cloth needs were still being imported. When imports declined sharply during the war, the government devised plans to increase cotton production. New legislation relaxed the restrictions on overtime, on child labor and on women's work. But, despite some success, the government was unable to increase textile production to fully compensate for the decline in imports.[73] In addition to textiles, increases were registered in iron and steel, sugar, and cement production. All the gains were due to state manufacturing, which seems to have increased its output by fifty to sixty percent between 1938 and 1946.[74] Larger private manufactures did not register any growth, while there might have been some growth in certain small manufacturing sectors. One source estimates that the growth rate of twelve percent per annum in medium and large industry during 1930–39 declined to five percent for 1939–45, all due to the state sector.[75]

The war years also witnessed a Wealth Levy (*Varlık Vergisi*) supposedly designed to tax extraordinary profiteering during wartime, such as by merchants and government contractors. Inaugurated in 1942, at the height of German influence, its application was left to local commissions with the guideline that non-Muslims were to be taxed ten times as much as Muslims, and *dönmes* twice as much. Regardless of its actual economic impact, which in some cases meant the bankruptcy of businessmen who could not raise the cash needed, the message rang clear and the post-war years witnessed departures of Greek and Jewish merchants and industrialists from İstanbul.[76] Although not actually eradicated, neither the non-Muslim bourgeoisie nor the Salonican group were likely any longer to make an impact on the post-war evolution of the bourgeoisie.

DEVELOPMENTS AFTER WORLD WAR II

The war years had created a ground swell of resentment against the government and its economic policies, especially among peasants who had borne the weight of mobilization and of forced purchases. One significant feature of the post-war conjuncture was, of course, the emergence of the U.S. and its espousal of the free market. The Turkish government quickly adjusted to the new scene and dismantled the war economy; the political balance rapidly shifted to favor private accumulation. Although investment in state enterprises did not decline, the public sector was relegated to subordinate status. All restrictions on private manufacturing investment were lifted. The best-positioned group to engage in private initiative were businessmen who had achieved a certain level of accumulation under the state-dominated economy. They allied themselves with directors and engineers who had gained their managerial and technical experience in the state sector, offered them partnerships, and thus preserved their access to the higher echelons of the bureaucracy. They also served a crucial political role in pressuring the single party to respond to the international conditions characterizing the post-1945 world. Koç, who best exemplifies the process of private accumulation through the graces of the state, and who sired the largest business conglomerate in Turkey, had discovered the benefits of the American connection quite early.[77] Others, such as the provincial merchants who had accumulated considerable wealth in the war, joined him in calling for a political regime that could accommodate the U.S. willingness to underwrite capitalist development in Turkey.

The U.S., on its part, actively pursued the installation of a new economic policy favoring the private sector. American experts prepared reports demonstrating the economic duality that state enterprise had engendered.[78] They argued that room should be made for a dispersed pattern of accumulation starting with agriculture and consumer-oriented industry. The bulk of the American funds went to constructing highways and importing agricultural machinery, all designed to boost economic growth outside the reach of the state administration. Investment in agriculture created boom conditions in the economy and a market for manufactures that the aspiring bourgeoisie wanted to tap. Perhaps more importantly, it unleashed a migration out of rural areas which populated the cities with 'free' labor.[79] The supply of labor had always been a problem for the manufacturing sector; now the problem was solved thanks to the transformation of the agricultural sector.

The world context presents the national arena with a set of opportunities, but whether these will be seized or not depends on the presence of social forces adequate to the task. In 1948, the Turkish bourgeoisie began to ask for an end to statist policies.[80] A wide political front—consisting of workers whose real incomes had declined thirty to fifty percent during the war, of commercialized peasantry who had suffered the consequences of mobilization, taxation and forced sales in the War, and the members of the public-private nexus who now felt ready to make it on their own—unseated the single-party regime in 1950 and brought the liberal Democrat Party to power. The turn away from statism in the 1950s succeeded precisely because there was a structural fit between the social transformation desired by dominant social forces and the agenda set by the world hegemonic power. American hegemony, complete with its international institutions, was not in and of itself the determinant of particular outcomes as they occurred in individual countries. Yet the opportunity space it created was a powerful inducement toward a specific type of development that would successfully tap the new potential.

This inducement often became quite concrete as dollar funds were allocated to aspiring manufacturers. Part of the American economic aid package had been earmarked for manufacturing development. In the 1950s, before the state-orchestrated policy of import-substitution came into effect, U.S. policy was oriented toward limiting public sector presence and boosting the private sector. Toward this end, the World Bank (I.B.R.D.) organized the establishment of the Industrial Development Bank of Turkey in 1950, to act as an intermediary in extending the foreign exchange credits made available by the World Bank and other international organizations.[81] Only private manufacturing projects would be funded. In a world where foreign exchange was scarce and every manufacturing undertaking required imported machines, technology, and inputs, these dollar credits became the *sine qua non* of successful investment. At the same time, manufacturers deemed worthy of credit gained an immediate advantage. By 1955, this bank was financing (mostly on a continuing basis through share participation) 293 projects.[82]

Developments of the 1950s constituted a structural transformation that left behind much of the previous class of businessmen while a new group of entrepreneurs emerged. It was no longer sufficient or even desirable to be identified with etatism. Most entrepreneurs who initially accumulated within the public-private nexus were able to make the transition, some could not.

As already mentioned, non-Muslim businessmen who had been alienated through the war-time policies of the government had begun to leave the country after 1945. The foundation of the Israeli state attracted some of the Jewish population, although not the wealthier families. Incidents in 1955 and political conflict with Greece led to the departure of Greeks and to the attrition of the İstanbul Greek community. Of the entire non-Muslim group of businessmen, only a small number of Jewish families maintained their relative status in the economy. This judgment applies to old Muslim-owned İstanbul merchant houses as well. A few of these made the transition, but the transfer of commercial accumulation to manufacturing mostly proved difficult. The Salonican groups had enjoyed a head start in manufacturing and had been singled out as the recipients of the first World Bank funds to be distributed to the private sector in 1950. Yet, they too remained within the confines of their initial textile investments. From being the wealthiest manufacturers in İstanbul during the early 1930s, they were reduced to the status of small suppliers who catered to old markets. By contrast, newcomers to the textile sector fared much better.

The end of the war witnessed a migration of newly wealthy provincial merchants to İstanbul. Foremost were those from Adana. In fact, the Çukurova region received another flow of wealth when tractors arrived to extend cultivation, and cotton prices jumped during the Korean War boom. This accumulation led to unprecedented prosperity in the cotton-related economy, which eventually was translated into finance and manufacturing capital. One structural innovation of this provincial invasion was the formation of a number of banks rivalling the financing monopoly of the major public-private bank. The *Yapı ve Kredi*, *Garanti*, and *Akbank*, which became the largest private banks in Turkey, were products of these formative years. These banks became the financial bureaus of their respective business groups whose principal investments were in manufacturing.[83] During the 1950s the number of larger private manufacturing concerns (employing ten or more) increased from 2,515 to 6,639. These employed 190,600 workers in 1961, compared to state enterprises which employed 126,200.[84]

The year 1950 was a watershed in the development of Turkish capitalism and in the transformation of manufactures. After the break of the 1950s, the transitions to successive stages of accumulation went more smoothly and the circulation of groups became less discontinuous. Light manufactures in the 1950s yielded to capital goods production in the 1960s and consumer durables in the 1970s. Until the late 1970s, manufacturing production grew at an annual rate of eight to twelve percent. The major investors were the same groups who had burst upon the scene at the end of World War II. They benefited from the continuity in the world environment which insured the extension of the boom into the 1970s. Although beset by the usual cyclical problems and frictions within the political process, Turkey's development had acquired a predictable momentum after the 1950s. To be sure, a more planned import substitution starting in the 1960s required greater involvement of the administrative apparatus in economic policy making and a greater degree of bureaucratic autonomy. The broad foundations governing the evolution of the bourgeois class, however, already had been laid and the principal actors remained on the stage.[85]

CONCLUSION

The development of manufacturing during the first half of the twentieth century was shaped by two peculiarities of the Turkish social formation. One was the large-scale elimination of the non-Muslim bourgeoisie during the transition from Empire to nation-state. I have already argued that the consequences of this discontinuity on the mode of formation of a manufacturing class, and on its relations with the state, were major. The second had to do with the nature of the agrarian structure, and the constraints this structure imposed on the development of manufactures.

Since early in the nineteenth century, small holdings had dominated the countryside in Anatolia. In addition to this structural feature, the demographic setback of the World War and its aftermath had led to a relative withdrawal of the peasants from the market, which was exacerbated by the crisis of the 1930s. The result was the economic closure of most Anatolian villages. This isolation made manifest the difficulty of a symbiotic devlopment between the growing manufacturing sector and the agrarian world. Since there was no concentration in land, accumulation in agriculture did not become a source of investment in manufacturing.

In the absence of agrarian-based wealth, formation of urban capital generally, and accumulation in manufacturing in particular, were more than usually vulnerable to events such as wars and population movements, and to state policy. Entrepreneurs rose and declined on the basis of their urban ventures; they had no surplus-producing property base to which they could retreat. For the same reasons, the state could take on such a prominent role in initiating and directing the course of the accumulation process. The urban bourgeoisie did not enjoy (until much later) either an economic or a political power base autonomous of state intervention. They had to accept their subordination to the state in order to proceed with their accumulation. In the 1930s and during the war years, severe economic depression and forced isolation from the world market delayed their eventual liberation from state subordination by two decades.

The relative poverty and absence of accumulation in the agrarian sector also determined the largely inconsequential nature of rural industry. There were no regions in Anatolia (akin to proto-industrial regions in Europe) that transformed under new economic conditions to emerge as industrial growth poles. When private investment began to dominate after 1950, small manufactures in cities and towns of Anatolia were driven out of the market, and there emerged a highly uneven concentration of manufactures, dominated by the İstanbul region, with İzmir and Adana following as distant competitors.

Agrarian technology and productivity remained unchanged during most of the period. Conditioned by a stable structure of agrarian property, and by the economic difficulties of World War II years, this relatively stagnant rural society did not yield migration until the 1950s. Hence, the formation of an urban industrial proletariat occurred rather late. "Free" labor, dispossessed of rural property, was not to come into existence until the 1960s. The absence of a proletariat implied that capitalists did not easily have access to an industrial labor force which could be instilled with the requisite work discipline.

It was also the case that villagers did not become significant consumers of urban manufactures until the 1950s. Until then, both the degree of commercialization and the consumption potential of the Anatolian peasant remained meager; urban manufacturers perforce catered to urban consumers. The national market (outside the urban areas) for the products of the manufacturing sector was both narrow and thin.

The 1950s ushered in solutions to most of the problems identified here. American hegemony ideologically strengthened the private sector and direct economic assistance contributed to its accumulation process. Businessmen began to acquire a degree of autonomy from the state. The agrarian transformation helped create a middle peasantry who began to accumulate and eventually constituted an internal market for an expanding manufacturing sector. Mechanization of agriculture and infrastructural investment towards the integration of the national market made peasants leave their villages to form an urban proletariat through migration. With the principal constituents of capitalist development in place, the state no longer enjoyed the autonomy to practice economic policies that fell outside the broad structural requirements of private accumulation. Since the 1950s, therefore, Turkey's transformation under capitalism, and the development of its manufacturing sector have occurred within a radically different set of parameters. Constraints and opportunities have shifted location: they no longer result from the peculiarities of the historical inheritance of Turkish society or from the autonomously generated policies of the state. Now, they derive overwhelmingly from the modalities of Turkey's insertion into the world economy and the inter-state system.

NOTES

1. Baer (1970), Akarlı (1983).

2. Kurmuş (1974), Kurmuş (1981).

3. Önsoy (1988), Toprak (1986).

4. Keyder (1990).

5. Keyder (1983).

6. Pamuk (1987).

7. Sussnitzki (1966).

8. Kasaba (1988).

9. Keyder (1987).

10. Toprak (1982).

11. McCarthy (1983).

12. Ökçün (1971).

13. Keyder (1981), chapter 2.

14. Ağaoğlu (1939), 149.

15. Soral (1974).

16. Owen (1984) is an argument establishing this point.

17. Quataert (1988).

18. Quataert (1983).

19. Pentzopoulos (1962).

20. Shorter (1985).

21. McCarthy (1983).

22. Information concerning the silk industry is found in various issues of the *Revue Commerciale du Levant, Bulletin Mensuel de la Chambre de Commerce Française de Constantinople*, (1914–1924), numbers 324–376.

23. Dalsar (1960).

24. Eldem (1970), 118.

25. Toprak (1982).

26. Ahmad (1980).

27. Eldem (1973), 40.

28. This report, "Industry in İzmir and the Greek Asia Minor, an Economic Study", was written by George Trakakis, an employee of the National Bank of Greece. This bank had a branch office in İzmir which, after May 1919, began to function in the capacity of a bureau assisting the Greek Administration of the occupied territories. The Office of the High Commissioner asked an Inspector of the National Bank to prepare a report on the industrial situation of the territory under occupation. The original typescript is in Greek and is in the library of the National Bank of Greece. It was translated into English by E. Florescu. One copy is deposited at the Middle East Center Library, St Antony's College, Oxford; there is another copy at the Fernand Braudel Center at Binghamton University.

29. See Karpat (1985) for population figures.

30. Eldem (1973), 37, also Ökçün (1970), introduction.

31. Toprak (1982), 191.

32. Keyder (1981), 60.

33. Keyder (1981), 59–62; Ökçün (1971).

34. Calculated from Eldem (1973), 43 and DIE (1969).

35. Eldem (1973), 43.

36. DIE (1969).

37. These are corrected figures. Official figures underestimate exports and exaggerate the deficit. See Keyder (1981): chapter 4.

38. İlkin (1978), 277.

39. Tahsin and Saka (1929) and (1930).

40. Başar (1945).

41. Tahsin and Saka (1929), 324 ff.

42. Hines et al. (1936), II, 259–60.

43. DİE (1969), 12–15.

44. Bayar (1939), 83.

45. Tekeli and İlkin (1977) and (1982).

46. İnan (1972), Conker (1937).

47. For various and conflicting interpretations of etatism see Okyar (1965), Boratav (1981), and Birtek (1985).

48. Conker (1937), 179.

49. Singer (1977), 31.

50. Conker (1937), 179.

51. Rivkin (1965).

52. Conker (1937), 240.

53. United Nations (1958), 59.

54. Singer (1977), 3; Singer (1977), 70–71.

55. Walstedt (1985) is a comprehensive review of state enterprise investment and pricing practices.

56. In fact, in a sample of enterprises still surviving in 1970, seventy-four percent of those founded during the 1930s had been founded by bureaucrat entrepreneurs; Soral (1974), 36.

57. Eldem (1946), 73.

58. Osman (1935).

59. Ağaoğlu (1939), 107.

60. Hershlag (1958), 175.

61. Conker (1937), 100.

62. Eldem (1946), 77–85.

63. DİE (1969).

64. Cillov (1954).

65. It must be mentioned that I have very little faith in census data. Categories seem to change at each census, and often it is difficult to understand the definitions. Problems with covering the entire population in a given category are well known. The figures cited in this paper should not be taken to reflect anything more than a rough order of magnitude.

66. There is no sociological study of the *dönme* community in İstanbul. For general information, articles in *Encyclopedia Judaica* are useful. An early study in Turkish which is less biased than most is Gövsa (1940).

67. Tanju (1983).

68. Eldem (1970), 131; Eldem (1973), 43.

69. Tekeli and İlkin (1986).

70. Singer (1977),17–18; United Nations (1958), 11.

71. Pamuk (1988).

72. United Nations (1958), 7.

73. Tekeli and İlkin (1986).

74. United Nations (1958), 97; Tekeli and İlkin (1986).

75. United Nations (1958), 17.

76. Clark (1972).

77. Koç (1973).

78. Thornburg (1949).

79. Keyder (1987), chapter 6.

80. See the collection of addresses and papers delivered at the 1948 Congress, Türkiye İktisat Kongresi (1948).

81. Singer (1977), 256–59.

82. United Nations (1958), 75; Chenery et al. (1953), 165–66.

83. For an informative account of the 'holding companies', see Sönmez (1990).

84. Singer (1977), 300.

85. For an analysis of the post-1950 process of industrialization see Keyder (1987), chapters 6–8.

REFERENCES CITED

Ağaoğlu, Samet
  1939   *Küçük Sanat Meseleleri, Türkiye'de ve Başka Yerlerde.* İstanbul.

Ahmad, Feroz
  1980   "Vanguard of a Nascent Bourgeoisie: The Social and Economic Policy of the Young Turks 1908–1918" in O. Okyar and H. İnalcık eds., *Social and Economic Policy of Turkey, 1081–1971.* Ankara.

Akarlı, Engin Deniz
  1983   "The uses of law among İstanbul artisans and tradesmen: The story of Gedik as implements, mastership, shop usufruct and monopoly, 1750–1850", paper presented at the International Symposium on Legalism and Political Legitimation in the Ottoman Empire and the Early Turkish Republic, Berlin.

Baer, Gabriel
  1970   "The Administrative, Economic and Social Functions of Turkish Guilds", *International Journal of Middle East Studies*, I, 1.

Başar, Ahmet Hamdi
  1945   *Atatürkle Üç Ay ve 1930'dan Sonra Türkiye.* İstanbul.

Bayar, Turgut
  1939   *La Türkiye İş Bankası.* Montreux.
Birtek, Faruk
  1985   "The Rise and Fall of Etatism in Turkey, 1932–1950," *Review*, VIII, no. 3.

Boratav, Korkut
1981   "Kemalist Economic Policies and Etatism" in Kazancigil, Ali and E. Özbudun eds.

Chenery, Hollis, G.E. Brandow, and E.J. Cohn
1953   "Turkish Investment and Economic Development" mimeo, Ankara: USA Operations Mission for Turkey.

Cillov, Haluk
1954   "Türkiye'de Sanayi İstatistikleri," *İstanbul Üniversitesi İktisat Fakültesi Mecmuası*, XVI, nos. 1–4.

Clark, Edward C.
1972   "The Turkish Varlık Vergisi Reconsidered," *Middle Eastern Studies*, May.

Conker, Orhan
1937   *Redressement Économique et Industrialisation de la Nouvelle Turquie.* Paris.

Dalsar, Fahri
1960   *Türk Sanayi ve Ticaret Tarihinde Bursa'da İpekçilik.* İstanbul.

DİE
1969   *Sanayi Sayımı 1927.* Ankara.

Eldem, Vedat
1946   "Le progrès de l'industrialisation en Turquie", *Revue de la Faculté des Sciences Économiques de l'Université d'Istanbul*, VIII, nos. 1–4.

Eldem, Vedat
1970   *Osmanlı İmparatorluğunun İktisadi Şartları Hakkında bir Tetkik.* İstanbul.
Eldem, Vedat
1973   "Mütareke ve Milli Mücadele Yıllarında Osmanlı İmparatorluğu Ekonomisi," paper presented at Türkiye İktisat Tarihi Semineri, Hacettepe University, Ankara.

Gövsa, İbrahim Alaettin
    1940   *Sabatay Sevi.* İstanbul.

Hershlag, Zvi Y.
    1958   *Turkey: An Economy in Transition.* The Hague.

Hines, W.D. et al.
    1936   *Türkiye'nin İktisadi Bakımdan Umumi Bir Tetkiki 1933–1934,* vols 1–3, Ankara.

İlkin, Selim
    1978   "Devletçilik döneminin ilk yıllarında işçi sorununa yaklaşım ve 1932 İş Kanunu Tasarısı," in İlkin 1978.

İlkin, Selim ed.
    1978   *Middle East Technical University Studies in Development* (Special Issue).

İnan, Afet
    1972   *Devletçilik İlkesi ve Türkiye Cumhuriyetinin Birinci Sanayi Planı.* Ankara.

Issawi, Charles
    1966   *The Economic History of the Middle East, 1800–1914.* Chicago.

Issawi, Charles
    1980   "De-industrialization and Re-industrialization in the Middle East since 1800", *International Journal of Middle East Studies,* XII, 4.

Karpat, Kemal H.
    1985   *Ottoman Population 1830–1914, Demographic and Social Characteristics.* Madison, Wisconsin.

Kasaba, Reşat
    1988   *The Ottoman Empire and the World Economy.* Albany.

Kazancıgil, Ali and E. Özbudun eds.
    1981   *Atatürk. Founder of a Modern State.* Hamden.

Keyder, Çağlar
    1981   *The Definition of a Peripheral Economy: Turkey 1923–1929.* Cambridge.

Keyder, Çağlar
    1983   "The Genesis and Structure of Small Peasant Ownership in Agriculture," *Review*, VII, 1.

Keyder, Çağlar
    1987   *State and Class in Turkey.* London.

Keyder, Çağlar
    1990   "Creation and Destruction of Forms of Manufacturing: the Ottoman Example," in Jean Batou ed. *Failed Attempts at Industrialisation in the Periphery.* Geneva.

Koç, Vehbi
    1973   *Hayat Hikayem.* İstanbul.

Kurmuş, Orhan
    1974   *Emperyalizmin Türkiye'ye Girişi.* İstanbul.

Kurmuş, Orhan
    1981   "Some Aspects of Handicrafts and Industrial Production in Anatolia," *Asian and African Studies*, XV, 1.

McCarthy, Justin
    1983   "Foundations of the Turkish Republic: Social and Economic Change", *Middle Eastern Studies*, April.

Ökçün, A. Gündüz ed.
    1970   *Osmanlı Sanayii: 1913, 1915 Yılları Sanayi İstatistiki.* Ankara.

Ökçün, A. Gündüz (1971), *1920–1930 Yılları Arasında Kurulan Türk Anonim Şirketlerinde Yabancı Sermaye Sorunu.* Ankara.

Okyar, Osman
    1965   "The Concept of Etatism", *Economic Journal*, March.

Önsoy, Rifat
    1988   *Osmanlı Sanayii ve Sanayileşme Politikası.* Ankara.

Osman, Mukdim
    1935   "L'artisanat en Turquie," *Revue Internationale de Travail,* Geneve.

Owen, Roger
    1984   "The Study of Middle Eastern Industrial History: Notes on the Interrelationship between Factories and Small-scale Manufacturing with Special References to Lebanese silk and Egyptian Sugar, 1900–1930," *International Journal of Middle East Studies,* XVI, 4.

Pamuk, Şevket
    1987   *The Ottoman Empire and European Capitalism, 1820-1913.* Cambridge.

Pamuk, Şevket
    1988   "War, State Economic Policies and Resistance by Agricultural Producers in Turkey, 1939–1945," *New Perspectives on Turkey,* II, no. 1.

Pentzopoulos, Dimitri
    1962   *The Balkan Exchange of Minorities and its Impact upon Greece,* Paris.

Quataert, Donald
    1983   "The Silk Industry of Bursa, 1880–1914", *Collection Turcica,* 1.

Quataert, Donald
    1988   "Ottoman Handicrafts and Industry in the Age of imperialism," *Review,* XI, 2.

Revue Commerciale du Levant

Rivkin, M.D.
    1965   *Area Development for National Growth: The Turkish Precedent.* New York.

Shorter, Frederic C.
    1985   "The Population of Turkey after the War of Indepen-
             dence," *International Journal of Middle East Studies*, XVII.
             No. 4.

Singer, Morris
    1977   *The Economic Advance of Turkey, 1938–1960*. Ankara.

Soral, Erdoğan
    1974   *Özel Kesimde Türk Müteşebbisleri*. Ankara.

Sönmez, Mustafa
    1990   *Kırk Haramiler, Türkiye'de Holdingler*. İstanbul, 4th
             printing.

Sülker, Kemal
    1976   *Türkiye'de İşçi Hareketleri*. İstanbul, 3rd printing.

Sussnitzki, A. J.
    1966   "The Ethnic Division of Labor" in Issawi (1966).

Tahsin, H. and R. Saka
    1929   *Sermayenin Şirketlerdeki Hareketi*. İstanbul.

Tahsin, H. and R. Saka
    1930   *Sermaye Hareketi*. İstanbul.

Tanju, Sadun
    1983   *Hacı Ömer*. İstanbul.

Tekeli, İlhan and Selim İlkin
    1977   *1929 Dünya Buhranında Türkiye'nin İktisadi Politika
             Arayışları*. Ankara.

Tekeli, İlhan and Selim İlkin
    1981   *Para ve Kredi Sisteminin Oluşumunda bir Aşama: T.C.
             Merkez Bankası*. Ankara.

Tekeli, İlhan and Selim İlkin
    1982   *Uygulamaya Geçerken Türkiye'de Devletçiliğin Oluşumu*.
             Ankara.

Tekeli, İlhan and Selim İlkin
  1986   "Savaşmayan Ülkenin Savaş Ekonomisi: Üretimden Tüketime Pamuklu Dokuma", paper presented at Türk Tarih Kongresi, 22–26 September, Ankara.

Thornburg, Max et al.
  1949   *Turkey, An Economic Appraisal.* New York.

Toprak, Zafer
  1982   *Türkiye'de 'Milli İktisat'.* Ankara.

Toprak, Zafer
  1986   "Tanzimat'ta Osmanlı Sanayii", *Tanzimat'tan Cumhuriyet'e Türkiye Ansiklopedisi*, V, pp. 1345–47.

Trakakis, George
  ca. 1920 "Industry in İzmir and the Greek Asia Minor, an Economic Study." İzmir.

Türkiye İktisat Kongresi
  1948   *Türkiye İktisat Kongresi (22–27 Kasım), Kongre Bülteni.* İstanbul.

United Nations
  1958   *The Development of Manufacturing Industry in Egypt, Israel and Turkey.* New York: UN Department of Economic and Social Affairs.

Walstedt, Bertil
  1985   *State Manufacturing Enterprise in a Mixed Economy. The Turkish Case.* Baltimore.

6

Afterword

Donald Quataert

The preceding contributions, it seems to me, have summarized the state of the art, pointed out the directions that future research must take, and situated the Ottoman/Turkish manufacturing experience in the global context so that fruitful comparative analyses can be attempted.

The contributions together suggest the character of Ottoman/Turkish manufacturing in its many forms as well as its persistence and its evolution over time. We found a full range of industrial organizations, ranging from those with independent artisans to merchant-dominated artisans to state-controlled workers. Hereafter, it is no longer possible to view the Ottoman/Turkish economy as a mere agrarian structure full of tilling cultivators. The rich details offered in the preceding pages make clear the complexity of that economy, replete with full-time manufacturers as well as artisan-cultivators and manufacturer-miners.

The volume should confirm and promote the growing conviction among specialists that the Ottoman experience, including that in manufacturing, was not *sui generis*. Rather, it represents a path taken that has important similarities as well as often subtle differences with patterns of change elsewhere in the world. While the blend of variables is unique to the Ottoman case, their blending represents a tinge along the multi-hued spectrum of global manufacturing possibilities. These variables include natural resources, market size, and state intervention. For example, take the Ottoman resource base. From a global perspective, it possessed relatively good supplies of the various textile fibers. But, on the other hand, water resources were far less abundant and became still scarcer thanks to the territorial losses of the imperial state. Or, consider the size of the domestic market; we have seen that it paled before its Chinese contemporary throughout the period. But still, the Ottoman domestic market 1550–1800 was far larger than that of England, France, or any of the German kingdoms. During this era, one could argue, manufacturers in the various states competed on the basis of relative equality. But, by 1900, the aggregate Ottoman domestic market was much smaller than that of contemporary Britain, France, or Germany. Or, take the role of the state. In ca. 1600, for example, it was very much greater in the Ottoman Empire than in the contemporary Moghul Empire in India; in 1900, the Ottoman state was far less interventionist than the Japanese.

Thus, we understand better the similarities and differences among the various manufacturing economies. And yet, we are far from understanding the actual reasons for the relative successes and failures of those economies. While we have begun to describe the workings of Ottoman manufacturing, our understanding of these dynamics is weak indeed.

The research agenda remains very full. We must continue, I believe, to seek to place the Ottoman state in the background of the manufacturing picture and give greater weight to the other variables at work. We continue to exaggerate the ability of the state to project its power. And yet, I also would argue that we need to treat the state in a more sophisticated fashion and to look more carefully at its interaction with those other variables. The state, afterall, is multi-leveled and quite different, both over time and in the various regions of the empire.[1]

Another important contribution of the volume has been the identification of regions or towns that were important at varying points in time. In fact, however, we often know little beyond the fact that manufacturing persisted at a particular location. We now need some solid local histories to rigorously analyze the changing character of production and trace the evolution of such manufacturing centers over time. As a corollary, we need to further pursue the issue of production networks, how merchants directed the flow of raw and semi-processed materials and connected artisans in many different regions with one another. And, it seems crucial to be more aware of the impact of frontier changes on Ottoman manufacturers. The cause-effect relationship between imperial military and economic power needs much further development.

NOTE

1. Derived from Frank Perlin's commentary.

Index

aba 69; *see also* woolen cloth

absenteeism 143, 147

acemi oğlan, as bound labor 19, 28, 37–38, *see also* janissary, candidate

Adana 142, 152, cotton industry 10, 88, 150; rise of 145–46; yarn factories 93, 94, 96

Aegean coastland 78, 81, 13132; cotton industry 39, 40, 48 n 118; migration 32

Aintab 38; lacemaking 103–04; textile industry 89, 100, 102

alcohol distilling 136

Aleppo 4, 21, 98; cotton industry 14, 89, 95, 96, 98, 100–02, 103; rug making 110; silk industry 104–05

Algiers, slave craftsmen 22–24

alizarin 89, 100; *see also* dyestuffs

alum 35, 77; *see also* dyestuffs

Amasya, silk industry 105

Anatolia 40, 43, 126, 127, 152; carpet and rug making 108–11, 144; cloth production 99–101; cotton production 88; population 132; slave labor 21; textile trade 14; wool production 98; yarn spinning 94

angora, textiles 14; wool 69

aniline 89, 100; *see also* dyestuffs

animal, husbandry and rural industry 64; skins and hides 39, 96

Ankara 21, 41, 145; cloth weaving factory 141; government 138, 144, 146; mohair industry 14, 38

Arapkir, cloth manufacturing 95, 99, 100, 115 n 55

Armenian community 128, 129, 134, 139; girls in rug industry 110; impact on manufacturing of expulsion of 129–132, 137; as intermediaries 127; landlords 145–146; manufacturers 93, 125

arms industry 60, 67

army, provisioning 15, 17–19, 24, 35, 36, 43, 69, 133, 141

Arsenal 16, 34; **acemi oğlan** 37; draftees 26–28; and sail cloth manufacture 78, 81; slave labor 23; of Tunis 45 n 36

artisan 13, 14, 16, 18–19, 26, 27, 31, 32, 36–38, 39, 40, 63, 67, 131, 144; civilian 38–40; drafted 24–26, 28–29, 43; emigration 31; loans 34; and military campaigns 36; organization 62–63; silk 75, 76; slave 23–24; state 78; *see also* guild, worker, and labor